AMERICAN ★ HISTORY

The GREAT DEPRESSION
Worldwide Economic Crisis

By Siyavush Saidian

Portions of this book originally appeared in *The Great Depression* by Don Nardo.

LUCENT PRESS

Published in 2018 by
Lucent Press, an Imprint of Greenhaven Publishing, LLC
353 3rd Avenue
Suite 255
New York, NY 10010

Designer: Deanna Paternostro
Editor: Siyavush Saidian

Cataloging-in-Publication Data

Names: Saidian, Siyavush.
Title: The Great Depression: worldwide economic crisis / Siyavush Saidian.
Description: New York : Lucent Press, 2018. | Series: American history | Includes index.
Identifiers: ISBN 9781534561311 (library bound) | ISBN 9781534561328 (ebook)
Subjects: LCSH: Depressions–1929–Juvenile literature. | United States–Economic conditions–1918-1945–Juvenile literature. | United States–History–1933-1945–Juvenile literature.
Classification: LCC E806.S35 2017 | DDC 973.91–dc23

Printed in the United States of America

CPSIA compliance information: Batch #BS17KL: For further information contact Greenhaven Publishing LLC, New York, New York at 1-844-317-7404.

Please visit our website, www.greenhavenpublishing.com. For a free color catalog of all our high-quality books, call toll free 1-844-317-7404 or fax 1-844-317-7405.

Contents

Foreword

The United States is a relatively young country. It has existed as its own nation for more than 200 years, but compared to nations such as China that have existed since ancient times, it is still in its infancy. However, the United States has grown and accomplished much since its birth in 1776. What started as a loose confederation of former British colonies has grown into a major world power whose influence is felt around the globe.

How did the United States manage to develop into a global superpower in such a short time? The answer lies in a close study of its unique history. The story of America is unlike any other—filled with colorful characters, a variety of exciting settings, and events too incredible to be anything other than true.

Too often, the experience of history is lost among the basic facts: names, dates, places, laws, treaties, and battles. These fill countless textbooks, but they are rarely compelling on their own. Far more interesting are the stories that surround those

basic facts. It is in discovering those stories that students are able to see history as a subject filled with life—and a subject that says as much about the present as it does about the past.

The titles in this series allow readers to immerse themselves in the action at pivotal historical moments. They also encourage readers to discuss complex issues in American history—many of which still affect Americans today. These include racism, states' rights, civil liberties, and many other topics that are in the news today but have their roots in the earliest days of America. As such, readers are encouraged to think critically about history and current events.

Each title is filled with excellent tools for research and analysis. Fully cited quotations from historical figures, letters, speeches, and documents provide students with firsthand accounts of major events. Primary sources bring authority to the text, as well. Sidebars highlight these quotes and primary sources, as well as interesting figures and events. Annotated bibliographies allow students to locate and evaluate sources for further information on the subject.

A deep understanding of America's past is necessary to understand its present and its future. Sometimes you have to look back to see how to best move forward, and that is certainly true when writing the next chapter in the American story.

Setting the Scene:

1928
Conservative Republican Herbert Hoover is elected president of the United States.

1930
The unemployment rate in the United States nearly doubles as a result of the Great Depression; the federal government insists that the economy is fine.

1928 1929 1930 1932

1929
The American stock market crashes, plunging the country into the Great Depression.

BROOKLYN DAILY EAGLE
LATE NEWS
WALL ST. IN PANIC AS STOCKS CRASH
Attempt Made to Kill Italy's Crown Prince
Hollywood Fire Destroys Films Worth Millions
High Duty Group Gave $700,000 to Coolidge Drive

1932
A large group of combat veterans organize a march on Washington, D.C., hoping to receive their bonus payments from the government; Franklin Delano Roosevelt is elected president.

A Timeline

1933
President Franklin Roosevelt begins his first term as president and begins instituting the first of his New Deal programs to boost the American economy.

1939
World War II erupts in Europe, stimulating the American economy as manufacturing productivity increases.

1933 | 1936 | 1939 | 1941

1936
Franklin Roosevelt wins a second presidential election by a wide margin; more New Deal programs are passed.

1941
Japanese forces launch a surprise attack on an American naval base in Pearl Harbor, Hawaii; the United States declares war on Japan, joining the world war and signaling the decline of the Great Depression.

Introduction

A DISASTER

Every country around the globe has its share of highs and lows. There are times of prosperity and times of discontent. This is especially true of countries that run on a capitalist economy. This kind of economic system is based on the idea that the ability to sell goods rests in the hands of private merchants, and it allows for the free market to develop with little government interference. Throughout history, this kind of system has been known to operate on a cycle of booms, with widespread riches and a thriving middle class, and busts, with massive poverty and unemployment. For the most part, economists and governments try to make the bust periods shorter and less frequent and the boom periods longer and more prosperous. However, sometimes the market simply cannot sustain itself.

In the history of the United States, the economy has experienced this boom-bust cycle numerous times. One of the most recent bust periods, also called a recession, occurred between 2007 and 2008. During this financial crisis, hundreds of thousands of people lost their jobs, millions of people lost money, and nearly everyone was unhappy with the economy. The effects of this recession lasted for years, but despite its terrible scale and negative outcome, it is not the worst financial disaster to ever occur in America. The Great Depression, which lasted from 1929 to 1939, was undoubtedly the most devastating.

As government officials saw the 2007 economic collapse incoming, they did their best to prepare for it. Because of this, the effects of a total collapse were avoided, and though the financial impact was still large, it could have been much worse. The country was able to recover relatively quickly. The Great Depression, on the other hand, was a crippling disaster not just because of the initial economic failure, but also because it took a decade for the government to repair the market. After the stock market crashed, banks failed, and millions of people lost their jobs, there seemed to be little hope of a better life. One historian wrote, "for more than ten long years the American people suffered an economic crisis unlike any they had ever known or anticipated."[1] The United States was not put back on its economic tracks until 1941, as the country was preparing to enter World War II.

No Home Left

Though the decade-long Great Depression was a terrible economic disaster, the United States was eventually able to do more than just recover from it. The nation emerged after World War II as the richest country in the world, and it has remained at or near the top of global wealth rankings ever since. For generations, many Americans have known nothing except economic opportunity, prosperity, and a high standard of living. For the most part, even the nation's poorest citizens do not have to live through conditions nearly as desperate as those faced by more than 10 million Americans in the midst of the Great Depression.

It is often difficult for people today to truly understand the scope and horror of the Great Depression. Merely listing the numbers of people who lost their life savings, jobs, and homes is not enough. Statistics cannot adequately convey the levels of hardship that individuals and families across the country had to endure. Indeed, after so much time has passed, the only way that these events can be understood is through the personal memories and testimony of those who witnessed them firsthand.

Take, for example, the housing conditions during the crisis. Millions of Americans, both in cities and rural areas, lived in small, flimsy shacks. It was all they could afford. After touring the Alabama countryside in 1937, two visitors described the humble dwelling of a father, mother, and four children:

> *The cabin sits close to the ground, with a single layer of boards for a floor; one window, or rather window hole, in each room (no glass, a wooden shutter instead); a roof that leaks so badly that when the last baby was born, [the mother's bed] had to be moved three times; walls without paper or plaster, of course—indeed you can see daylight through their cracks.*[2]

The shack had no electricity, no running water, and no toilets, which was typical of poor, rural America at the time. Despite the terrible conditions, this family at least had a roof over its head. At the height of the Depression, Mary Owsley of Oklahoma reported,

> *[People were living] in everything from … houses built out of cardboard boxes and old pieces of metal … I knew one family there in Oklahoma City, a*

Millions of unemployed Americans were forced to live in shacks, similar to these, after the Great Depression struck.

> *man and a woman and seven children lived in a hole in the ground … They had chairs and tables and beds back in that hole. And they had the dirt all braced up there, just like a cave.*[3]

No Necessities

The horrible housing situation was only one of the many components of the crisis. Because of the widespread lack of both jobs and money, many parents could not afford to buy decent clothes for either themselves or their children. "My children have not got no shoes and clothing to go to school with," a father from West Virginia stated in 1935, "and we [have not] got enough bed clothes to keep us warm."[4]

Food was also difficult to come by in both cities and towns across the country. Various charities and religious institutions responded by setting up soup kitchens, where huge lines of hungry people formed every evening. Peggy Terry, a woman from Kentucky, later remembered,

Thousands of poor, unemployed people were forced into long lines just to get a meal during the Depression.

> *I first noticed the difference when we'd come home from school in the evening. My mother'd send us to the soup line ... If you happened to be one of the first ones in line, you didn't get anything but water that was on top. So we'd ask the guy who was ladling out the soup ... to please dip down to get some meat and potatoes from the bottom of the kettle.*[5]

In 1932, a secretary for the Community Council of Philadelphia testified before a Senate subcommittee about the horrible food situations he had witnessed:

> *One woman said she borrowed 50 cents from a friend and bought stale bread for 3 1/2 cents per loaf, and that is all [her family] had for eleven days except for one or two meals ...*

> *One woman went along the docks and picked up vegetables that fell from the wagons. Sometimes the fish vendors gave her fish at the end of the day. On two different occasions, the family was without food for a day and a half.*[6]

This was not unique to Philadelphia. A man living in a tenement apartment in New York City described a similarly desperate situation, and tried to improve his life by writing a letter to his Congressman in Washington, D.C.:

> *It is now nearly seven months I am out of work. I hope you will try to do something for me.... I have four children who are in need of clothes and food.... My daughter who is eight is very ill and not recovering. My rent is [over]due two months and I am afraid of being [evicted].*[7]

In fact, such threats of eviction were a real danger for common citizens during the Depression. In just 1932, more than 270,000 American families were forcibly removed from their homes because

Thousands of Americans were suddenly evicted from their residences when the Great Depression hit. Many had to choose between paying their rent and feeding their families.

they could not afford to pay their rent. Many of these now-homeless people ended up sleeping in alleyways, parks, or even garbage dumps, where they could huddle up near incinerators to keep warm.

Nowhere to Turn

Under such poor conditions, and with no end or remedy in sight, it is not surprising that many people eventually started to believe that the Depression would never end. Some people went so far as to take their own lives. Suicide rates increased 50 percent during the years of the Great Depression. One government relief worker reported in 1934 that almost every adult she aided had "talked of suicide at one time or another."[8] In that same year, a Pennsylvania man asked a local government official, "Can you be so kind as to advise me as to which would be the most [humane] way to dispose of my self and [my] family, as this is about the only thing that I see left to do. No home, no work, no money. We cannot go along this way."[9]

It is difficult for most modern Americans to imagine these levels of hardship and desperation. How did things get so bad in the United States? Could a similar massive economic catastrophe strike the country in the future? To answer these questions, it is important to examine how the Great Depression came to be, how the government responded to it, and how ordinary citizens adapted, survived, and set the economy back on the right track. It is also crucial to realize that, though the Depression itself ended, its legacy will live on. In the words of noted historian Robert McElvaine, "No period in American history has more … importance … than does the Depression decade. Events in those years have determined the direction of our social and economic policies, our relationship to our government, and our political alignment ever since."[10]

Chapter One

THE GREAT DEPRESSION BEGINS

The most basic cause of the Great Depression was an overall decrease in spending that occurred quickly. The most visible manifestation of this lack of spending was the terrible stock market crash of 1929. However, this was just one of the numerous unfortunate financial turns that initiated the Depression. Banks and stockbrokers had been investing dangerously for years (a practice called speculative investment), and the United States federal government was trying to pass new laws to protect the stock market. As these two sides fought one another, the more general economy was facing serious problems. Though these issues gradually worsened in the years leading up to the Depression, there were few steps taken to prevent it.

One of the reasons why the Depression struck quickly and unexpectedly is that many people thought that the economy was doing extremely well. Though many Americans were still poor, many more were able to enter the middle class. This was seen as undeniably positive by a large number of people. Historian Howard Zinn described this time:

> *Unemployment was down, from 4,270,000 [people] in 1921 to a little over 2 million in 1927. The general level of wages for workers rose. Some farmers made a lot of money. The 40 percent of all families who made over $2,000 a year could buy new gadgets: autos [cars], radios, refrigerators. Millions of people were not doing badly—and they could shut out of the picture the others—the tenant farmers ... [and] the immigrant families in the big cities either without work or not making enough to get the basic necessities.*[11]

In addition to this, the wealthiest class of society saw its fortunes grow even faster than the middle class. This would eventually come to harm the general state of the economy. However, because many people were now richer, they believed that the economy was in great shape. High-profile stockbrokers, who insisted that the stock market was going to be incredibly profitable, seemingly confirmed this. As a result, stock prices were at an all-time high in 1929, despite the government's attempt to keep prices down. However, this huge rise in stock prices is what eventually led to the crash, which is now remembered as Black Thursday and Black Tuesday. Though it is not possible to identify a single cause of the Great Depression, the speculative investment practices of banks were undoubtedly a major contributor.

The Wealth Gap Widens

Many historians point to the 1929 stock market crash as the primary cause of the Depression; however, it is also important to understand the other factors at work in the national economy around the same time. The wealth gap, or the gap between the richest portion of Americans and the poorest, started widening—and never stopped. A 1934 study conducted by the Brookings Institution, a social policy group, found a huge rift between rich and poor in pre-Depression America. In 1929, shortly before the stock market crash, 0.1 percent of American families held wealth and income equal to the entire bottom 42 percent of American families. Historian Robert McElvaine explained this statistic:

> *Stated in absolute numbers, approximately 24,000 families had a combined income as large as [the combined income of] more than 11.5 million poor and lower-middle-class families. Fully 71 percent of all American families ... had [yearly] incomes under $2,500. At the other extreme, the 24,000 richest families enjoyed annual incomes in excess of $100,000 and 513 American families ... reported incomes above $1 million ... nearly 80 percent of the nation's families—some 21.5 million households—had no savings whatsoever. The 24,000 families at the top—0.1 percent—held 34 percent of all savings.*[12]

This meant that a huge amount of wealth was being concentrated in the hands of a relatively tiny amount of people and families. Many of these families were the owners of massive businesses, such as the descendants of oil tycoon John D. Rockefeller or steel magnate Andrew Carnegie, and they employed millions of Americans. Big businesses were making the American economy boom, raising millions of people to the middle class, and improving the general quality of life nationwide. However, this kind of economic system has one flaw that, at the time, few economists, politicians, or advisors were able to identify. What would happen if some of these families or businesses lost their fortunes?

Because most of these companies employed tens of thousands of Americans, all of those people would lose their jobs if the company went under. In large-scale economics, someone losing a job is disastrous. That person is no longer creating anything to add to a nation's financial growth, and their ability to spend money is greatly diminished. If thousands of people lost their jobs all at once, there would be a noticeable decrease in economic development. Moreover, if a large company failed, the stock market would be impacted as well. Millions of stockholders could easily lose just as much money as someone who is suddenly unemployed.

Meanwhile, some wealthy investors increasingly engaged in risky business practices. Stock pools represented only one example of the stock market manipulation that was starting to become widespread in the late 1920s. Historian Samuel E. Morison described what a stock pool does:

> *A group of men would get together, buy a sizable block of stock of [anything], then trade shares back and forth, hiking the price and pulling*

This photgraph shows the crowds that gathered on Wall Street on Black Tuesday in 1929.

Unsustainable Policies

America was facing many internal economic problems—from the condition of the stock market to the emergence of dangerous business practices—but it also had external worries. Among these was a growing instability in trade relations between the United States and other nations, as explained by Robert McElvaine:

> *By the late twenties, each country was seeking to advance its own interests, even if in the process it worsened the positions of others. In a delicate, interdependent world economy, these "beggar thy neighbor" tactics were suicidal. Nowhere should this have been more clear than in the Untied States. This country was trying nothing less in the 1920s than to be the world's banker, food producer, and manufacturer, but to buy as little as possible from the world in return. This attempt to eat the world and have it, too, was ... a self-defeating policy [and] ... If the United States would not buy from other countries, there was no way for others to buy from Americans, or to meet interest payments on American loans.*
>
> *The weakness of the international economy and [unwise] American foreign policy unquestionably contributed to the coming of the Great Depression.*[1]

1. Quoted in Robert McElvaine, *The Great Depression: America 1929–1941*. New York, NY: Random House, 1993, p. 34.

> *in outsiders who hoped to get in on the profits. When the stock reached an agreed point, members of the pool dumped it on the market, took their profits, and retired, leaving the suckers to take the [loss].*[13]

The federal government was actively attempting to stop this kind of market manipulation in the 1920s. Powerful stockbrokers worked around the new laws by increasingly making risky financial ventures. One common investment before the Depression was in a holding company. Holding companies do not make a product or provide a service. Rather, the operators of a holding company buy several other businesses and manage them, taking a percentage of the profit of each business. With few exceptions, wealthy individuals acquired and ran holding companies, in which hundreds of thousands of poorer, working-class people bought shares. This would ordinarily not be a problem, but at the time, many managers used immoral or illegal strategies to run the holding companies. They often mismanaged the companies while taking money from them to fill their own pockets.

Because of this poor management, such companies had a high risk of failure, and when they went out of business, they left the investors with a collection of worthless stocks, essentially having wasted their investment. As these weak companies increased in number, the risk of financial ruin to thousands of investors—and to the national economy—increased alongside them.

Waiting to Fail

These and other financial mistakes and shady business practices were not the only contributors to the stock market crash and the Depression. Several other factors included the increased production of goods, fluctuations in consumer spending and borrowing, and their effects on banks. For example, large American farms significantly increased their levels of production in the 1920s. Thinking that the economy would continue to expand, these wealthy farmers massively overproduced their goods. By doing this, they created a large surplus of crops and other

After the stock market crash of 1929, thousands of farms were forced to shut down all across the country.

farm products. This had the unintended effect of dramatically lowering the prices of these products. As a result, small farmers found it more difficult to make a profit, because they could not match the production of large corporate farms, and they faced an increased risk of bankruptcy if the economy suddenly slowed down.

Similarly, many manufacturing industries produced more goods than average Americans could afford to buy. Because of this nationwide surplus in 1928 and 1929, not long before the market crashed, these companies began cutting back their production. This inevitably meant laying off some of their workers. In turn, the people who lost their jobs had to reduce their spending, which increased the surplus of those goods, and thereby caused even more cutbacks in production and more job losses. This was a vicious cycle.

This negatively affected banks as well, partly because these now-unemployed people had to take from their savings, which decreased the amount of money banks could use to invest. Even more ominous for banks, though, was the worsening situation with credit and debt. Many struggling small farmers took out business loans, and millions of ordinary consumers bought goods on credit. Buying something on credit means that the purchaser (the borrower or debtor) takes out a small loan in order to afford the item, and slowly pays their lender (also called a creditor, typically their bank) back over time. By 1929, 60 percent of all automobiles and 80 percent of all radios were purchased on credit. Between 1925 and 1929, the amount owed to banks by borrowers more than doubled, from $1.4 billion to $3 billion. As unemployment increased, large numbers of people found themselves unable to pay back their debts. Without that income, many banks were on the verge of collapse, and some were already shut down before the 1929 market crash.

Radios were one of America's most popular household items in the early 20th century, and many were bought on credit. After the Depression hit, few families could afford to pay back their debts.

Though it appeared that the decade of the 1920s was a signal of good economic things to come, the economy was actually unstable beneath its rich exterior. In modern terms, the country was in an economic bubble. Eventually, the combined disasters of a stock market collapse, high unemployment, and widening wealth distribution, made the Great Depression inevitable. Journalist Edward R. Ellis, who lived through the Depression, summed up the economic climate:

> *Greedy people wanted more than they needed. Foolish people thought they could get something for nothing. Impulsive people bought now in the hope of paying later. Income and wealth were distributed unfairly and dangerously ... The masses were not paid enough money to consume all the goods they produced. The economy was unsound. The corporate structure was sick. The banking system was weak. Foreign trade was out of balance ... [These] conditions left the economy a flawed and loaded gun, and when the stock market crashed, the gun did not merely fire—it exploded in everyone's face.*[14]

Prosperity and Ruin

The great crash came after the New York Stock Exchange suffered a series of devastating blows over the course of several weeks. In October 1929, the market suddenly slumped when thousands of investors, worried that their stocks were declining in worth, sold them in large quantities. As more people dumped their stocks, a general panic set in, which led to the biggest mass sale of stock the country had ever seen. In fact, the stock sales were so numerous and huge that, by the end of the day, the ticker machine, which was used to record transactions, was running more than an hour behind actual sales times.

Ben Isaacs, a businessman from Chicago who went door-to-door selling clothes, later remembered the commotion: "I was going on my business and I heard the newspaper boys calling, running all around the streets and [yelling] stock market crashed, stock market crashed. [The news] came out just like lightning."[15]

The market panic continued in the days that followed. On Tuesday, October 29, the stock market lost an unprecedented $14 billion. The total amount of money lost during the decline of the pre-Depression stock market is the equivalent of hundreds of billion dollars in the 21st century. Immediately, Americans who owned a large amount of stock were hit with financial disaster. Some of them suffered such terrible losses that they took their own lives. Arthur A. Robinson, who was a wealthy businessman, later recalled what happened to a successful cigar company: "I got a call from the company president. Could I loan him $200 million? I refused, because at the time I had to protect my own [business]. His $115 stock dropped to $2 and

The New York Stock Exchange, shown here, was the site of a massive collapse in 1929.

he jumped out of the window of his Wall Street office."[16]

Another wealthy observer who managed to survive the crash intact, Sidney J. Weinberg, said, "I don't know anybody that jumped out of the window. But I know many who threatened to jump … These were people who were trading in the market or in banking houses. They broke down physically as well as financially."[17]

As time went on and the market did not show signs of improvement, the rich were not the only ones who experienced financial despair. The effects of the enormous losses in the stock market rapidly spiraled outward, engulfing most of the rest of society, as historian Gerald W. Johnson explained:

> *When the panic of 1929 suddenly wiped out the whole value of many stocks and sharply reduced the values of others, a great number of people who had thought themselves rich, or at least well-off, found themselves with much less than they had thought they had, or with nothing at all. By [the] millions they quit buying anything except what they had to save to stay alive. This drop in spending threw the stores into*

A Misguided Economy

When the stock market crashed in 1929, it was a difficult time for nearly everyone. Though Black Thursday and Black Tuesday (October 24 and 29, 1929) are the most famous dates, the decline took place over more than just two days. Moreover, people were slow to react to the market, because some economists and stockbrokers distributed misinformation. As explained by McElvaine,

> *[It was] a long, rolling downward slide that went on for weeks, from September 3 through November 13 [1929]. There were brief upsurges after some of the worst days.*

> *The ... boom was, of course, dependent upon confidence [in the economy] ... Even after the collapse had started in the fall on 1929, the demand for confident statements [about the stock market] kept bringing forth a plentiful supply ... As the decline degenerated into the Crash, a wide array of leaders repeated phrases containing the words "fundamentally sound."*[1]

1. Robert McElvaine, *The Great Depression: America 1929–1941*. New York, NY: Random House, 1993, p. 46.

> *trouble, and they quit ordering [new products] and [fired] clerks. When orders stopped, the factories shut down, and factory workers had no jobs.*[18]

This financial chain reaction was destructive to the national economy. As consumer buying significantly slowed down, many people were uncomfortable keeping their money in banks. Thousands of people withdrew their savings and hid them under their mattresses or in their attics. People also defaulted, which means failing to make payments, on their bank loans. Both of these trends fatally wounded hundreds of banks, which themselves went bankrupt and had to close down. When this occurred, the clients who had not yet withdrawn their savings lost them. The banks were no longer able to return their money, and no laws were in place to protect them. As banks failed, millions of people, who had not even lost their jobs, were thrown into poverty.

As the disastrous collapse hit, companies both big and small laid off large

Millions of Americans, who did not trust banks to keep their money safe, withdrew their savings and stockpiled the money. This caused thousands of banks to go out of business.

portions of their workforces. Unemployment rates, which had remained fairly low at under 5 percent in 1929, rose to 9 percent by early 1930. In the next 2 years, the rise continued and reached a devastating 25 percent. This was a worst-case scenario, because unemployment insurance and social security, which today help temporarily jobless people survive, did not exist at the time. The government had no safety measures in place to protect the people from this momentous collapse.

Begging for Relief

Ben Isaacs's clothing business was among those that suffered. Many of his customers, most of whom owed him money, could not afford to pay him. As he later recalled,

> *We lost everything. [Normally] I would collect four, five hundred dollars a week [from customers]. After [the crash], I couldn't collect fifteen, ten dollars a week. I was going around trying to collect enough money to keep my family going. It was*

Street Corner Salespeople

As the Great Depression continued into the 1930s, one of the famous images of the Depression appeared: a man, wearing a well-tailored suit, selling apples on a corner. After finding themselves unemployed, some people set up small wooden carts or stands on street corners in cities and towns all across America. They sold apples for a few cents each. These apple sellers came from all walks of life; before the Depression, they might have been bankers, farmers, lawyers, or teachers. In New York City, apple peddlers acquired their produce by lining up outside the Apple Growers Association on Harrison Street in Manhattan. On some days, when apples were more scarce, many of these desperate New Yorkers went away empty-handed.

Images of an unemployed man selling apples, such as this one, are some of the most familiar symbols of the Depression era.

impossible … We tried to struggle along living day by day. Then I couldn't pay the rent. I had a little car … I sold it for $15 in order to buy some food for the family … I didn't have a nickel in my pocket.[19]

Eventually, Isaacs had to go on relief, which means accepting handouts of money, food, and clothing from charities. However, because of the terrible conditions everywhere, even that did little to stop his family's downward slide:

I went to the relief and they … gave me $45 a month … So how long can that $45 go? I was paying $30 on the rent. I [had to] find another a cheaper [apartment], stove heat, for $15 a month … Today a dog wouldn't live in that type of a place. Such a dirty, filthy, dark place … About two months later, all of a sudden no water. The city closed for the [landlord's] non-payment of the water bill.

My wife used to carry two pails of water from the next-door neighbors and bring it up for us to wash the kids and to flush the toilet with it, and then wash our hands and face with it … we lived without water for almost two months.[20]

New York City was also drastically affected by the onset of the Great Depression. Hundreds of thousands of citizens lived in the same horrible conditions that Ben Isaacs's family did in Chicago. Struggling songwriter Yip Harburg witnessed the worsening plight of many of these down-and-out people:

I was walking along the street … and you'd see the bread lines … fellows with burlap on their shoes were lined up all along Columbus Circle, and went for blocks and blocks around the park, waiting … The prevailing greeting at that time, on every block you passed, by some poor guy coming up, was: "Can you spare a dime?" Or: "Can you spare something for a cup of coffee?"[21]

People all across America desperately wondered when the crisis would end, when life would get back to normal, and when people would regain their jobs, lives, and dignity. In May 1930, roughly seven months after the stock market crash and beginning of the Depression, President Herbert Hoover tried to raise people's spirits. "We have now passed the worst,"[22] he declared with confidence. At the time, the American people believed him; they had no other choice.

Chapter Two

A POWERLESS PRESIDENT

Throughout American history, there have been few presidents with a worse legacy than Herbert Hoover, who served from 1929 until 1933. Though he was elected to the presidency because he had an outstanding reputation—he did humanitarian work during World War I—after the stock market crashed near the beginning of his tenure, he was widely hated. Historians and economists have criticized him for not seeing the crisis coming and for not quickly or effectively addressing the nation's major economic concerns. His administration was unable to slow down, let alone stop, the disaster.

Most historians believe that President Herbert Hoover, shown here, did not do enough to prevent the Great Depression or repair the economy.

One of the biggest mistakes of Hoover's presidency was that he did not acknowledge the depth and severity of the Great Depression. While he could not avoid the fact that thousands of people were joining the ranks of the unemployed every day, he believed that the situation would simply resolve itself, given enough time. His top aides advised him that the market could heal on its own and that America would soon be back on its feet. However, this never came to pass. Just as stockbrokers were promising people that things were looking up, politicians were quick to declare that recovery had started. In 1930, despite high levels of unemployment and widespread poverty, Hoover's secretary of labor commented, "Courage and resource are already swinging us back on the road to recovery."[23]

Denying the Obvious

Because Hoover's top officials were hesitant to identify the Depression as a full-scale crisis, his administration was slow and ineffective in fighting against it. Though he did eventually break from top political leaders and attempt to stimulate the economy, the market was so thoroughly broken that none of his initiatives were much help. This is also partially because his relief efforts were aimed at helping banks and stocks, assuming that the improvement of these industries would lead to an improvement for everyone. Throughout his presidency, Hoover's administration took the stance that giving free aid to the American people would not help the economy—it would destroy it.

One of the reasons Hoover refused to help citizens at an individual level is that he believed it would weaken America's sense of spirit in the long term. America was a country whose foundations were in the power of the individual and the strength of the free market. Historian T.H. Watkins explained,

> *Hard work, honesty, and independence, [Hoover's administration] believed utterly, had brought [America] to the forefront of nations, had built a breed of [people] who had taken the institutions of the founding fathers and made them the wonder of the world.*
>
> *Anything that might weaken the strength of that tradition would weaken the very character of America and was ... evil. Government, charity, especially, by robbing people of initiative, would be the very embodiment of error. The national government should stay out of the personal lives of its citizens, even if they were in trouble.*[24]

Though this philosophy was meant to be better for American citizens in the long run, it was not at all helpful to people who were starving and homeless in 1930. Despite some conservative intervention by the federal government and the best efforts of business leaders nationwide, the stock market continued to suffer crashes, and the country's biggest industries were failing. The Great Depression was still at its beginning in the early 1930s, and the numbers of American poor and unemployed continued to grow.

A History of Self-Reliance

It is important to note that Hoover was neither a totally incompetent politician nor a cruelly insensitive person. He did what he truly believed would be the best for the American people. The problem with his presidency lies mostly with the fact that his economic philosophy simply did not work in the 1930s. It was founded on the ideas of individual hard work, a deregulated free market, and providing for the poor class of society through private charitable organizations.

Hoover's entire life before becoming president had been shaped by these and similar ideas. After graduating from Stanford University in 1895 with a degree in geology, he became a highly successful mining engineer. After making his fortune, he began devoting much of his time to relief work for people in need. He was particularly active in programs that fed homeless and starving Europeans during World War I. In 1917, President Woodrow Wilson put him in charge of food programs in the war effort. Hoover was a true humanitarian; he would provide aid to anyone who asked for it. He went so far as to supply food to millions of starving Russians in the aftermath of the Communist takeover in Soviet Russia. Americans, being firmly anti-Communist, widely criticized Hoover's charity. He defended himself by declaring, "Twenty million people are starving. Whatever their politics, they shall be fed!"[25]

After making a name for himself as a humanitarian in the early 1920s, Hoover served as secretary of commerce under

Hoover served as the secretary of commerce before becoming president, so many Americans believed that he would have a strong understanding of the national economy.

Presidents Warren G. Harding and Calvin Coolidge. In this new position, Hoover worked to create voluntary partnerships between government, big businesses, and major private charities. He was praised for coordinating relief efforts after disastrous floods ravaged the Mississippi valley in 1927. The following year, he ran for president, often saying in his speeches, "We in America today are nearer to the final triumph over poverty than ever before in the history of any land."[26]

In 1928, while he was on the campaign trail, this message rang loud and clear. Americans had been experiencing great prosperity for nearly a decade, and Hoover brought a promise of continued success. In the eyes of history, however, these words sound hollow. Not even a year into his presidency, the stock market collapsed, and millions of people became stricken with poverty. Regardless, he thoroughly believed that individuals, through personal ambition and hard work, could make poverty a thing of the past. He explained that philosophy in one of his most famous speeches, delivered in October 1928, shortly before the presidential election. America's social system, he said, "is founded upon the [idea] that only through ordered liberty, freedom and equal opportunity to the individual will his initiative and enterprise spur on the march of progress. And in our insistence upon equality of opportunity has our system advanced beyond all the world."[27]

This system worked so well, Hoover claimed, because the central government played a minimal role in business. This left private business owners and managers to hire and fire, manufacture and market goods, and invest well-earned capital, or money. For Hoover, this approach was only right for an independent, self-governing nation. In contrast, "When the federal government undertakes to go into commercial business," Hoover warned, "it immediately finds itself in a [maze], every alley of which leads to the destruction of self-government."[28] When big government tries to create and control industry and business, he believed, it robs individuals of the right to do so on their own. It also dangerously increases governmental power, potentially threatening people's liberty. Even after the initial onset of the Depression, the new president refused to waver from this basic philosophy of self-reliance and fear of big government intervention. In an early 1931 press statement, he said,

> *This is not an issue as to whether the people are going hungry or cold in the United States. It is solely a question of the best method by which hunger and cold can be prevented. It is a question as to whether the American people [or the Federal Treasury] … will maintain the spirit of charity and of mutual self help … If we break down this sense of responsibility, of individual generosity to individual … we have not only [harmed] something infinitely valuable in the life of the American*

Returning to the Land

Though President Herbert Hoover was the most prominent American to encourage the poor and homeless to return to a self-reliant lifestyle, he was far from the only one. Henry Ford, founder of the Ford Motor Company, wrote an essay in 1932 advising people to grow their own food to survive:

Henry Ford was one of the best businessmen in American history. During the Depression, he advised the unemployed to return to farming the land.

Methods of self-help are numerous and great numbers of people have made the stimulating discovery that they need not depend on employers to find work for them—they can find work for themselves … The land! That is where our roots are … From the land comes everything that supports life … The land has not collapsed or shrunk in either extent or productivity. It is there waiting to honor all the labor we are willing to invest in it … Let every man and every family at this season of the year cultivate a plot of land and raise a sufficient supply for themselves or others. Every city and village has vacant space whose use would be permitted.[1]

1. Henry Ford, "On Unemployment," *Literary Digest*, June 18, 1932.

people but have struck at the roots of self-government … I am confident that our people have the resources, the initiative, the courage, the stamina and [kindness] of spirit to meet this situation in the way they have met their problems over generations.[29]

Trying to Revive a Nation

Despite Hoover's traditional, conservative philosophy of government and economic affairs, he did not think that his administration should sit back forever and watch the crisis unfold. He simply felt that the government should only do things that were appropriate for it to do. Years earlier, when he was helping European refugees and American flood victims, he had organized and coordinated relief efforts by businesses, charities, and government agencies. Faced with the major economic downturn that followed the crash of 1929, he employed the same approach. Late that year, the president summoned leading industrialists and government officials to the White House. He tried to persuade most of them, including the wealthy car manufacturer Henry Ford, to consider not firing so many people and to not cut the wages of the employees they did keep. He believed this would give Americans the ability to spend, which could help fix the market. Hoover also spoke to the heads of the big utility companies about spending more on new construction programs. The hope was that this would create some much-needed positions that anyone could fill.

In addition, Hoover devoted a significant amount of time and energy to organizing charity drives. During the winter of 1929 to 1930, he made numerous appeals to wealthy Americans, big companies, and religious institutions, asking them to donate money and goods to the poor. This effort produced some contributions, but they were a tiny amount relative to the scope of the national crisis. Around this same time, some congressmen urged the president to launch relief efforts funded by the federal government. He repeatedly refused to do so.

Hoover also declined proposals that called for the government to create a large public works program to put people back to work. He called it "the most gigantic pork-barrel ever perpetrated by the American Congress."[30] The term "pork barrel" is a negative term that refers to inappropriate or inconsiderate government spending. Hoover did not believe that taxpayer money should be spent on putting unemployed people on the federal government's payroll.

Hoover and his advisers believed that a better way to repair the failing economy was to lower tariffs. Tariffs are the taxes that foreign countries and companies pay to the United States in order to sell their goods and services there. Hoover thought that lowering U.S. tariffs would encourage other countries to lower their own tariffs. If they did so, this could stimulate more international desire for American products and spur new production and create jobs at home. Congress, however, disagreed with this policy. The stock market crash of 1929 had prompted many politicians to believe that the only way to prosper again was to focus on America's economy—and to ignore the international community.

In June 1930, legislators passed the Smoot-Hawley Tariff Act. Designed to encourage the production and sale of domestic products in the United States,

Senators Willis C. Hawley (left) and Reed Smoot (right) were the sponsors of the Smoot-Hawley Tariff Act, which passed after the stock market crash.

Smoot-Hawley raised America's already-high import tariffs, imposing a tax of 60 percent or more on thousands of imported products. More than 1,000 economists saw the danger that Smoot-Hawley posed and signed a petition urging Hoover to veto the bill. Its supporters lobbied him aggressively, and he reluctantly signed it. The results, as the economists had predicted, were disastrous. Many foreign nations retaliated by raising their own tariffs, which discouraged global trade. Between 1929 and 1932, imports fell by two-thirds, and the revenue from exports dropped by billions of dollars.

Another Hoover initiative, which ended up backfiring, was the Revenue Act of 1932. It was a huge tax increase across all income levels, largely in the form of income taxes. Hoover intended this new tax rate to increase federal revenues, which would enable the government to possibly enact new social programs without ruining the budget. People with the highest incomes saw their taxes rise to an alarming 63 percent, while taxes levied on using checks or inheriting money were also heightened. Opposition to the Revenue Act was widespread throughout the country. These new taxes actually hurt the American economy; because people now had much less money, they were much less willing to spend it. When people do not spend, the economy comes to a halt.

One of the federal programs that the Revenue Act helped fund was the Reconstruction Finance Corporation (RFC), formed by Congress in 1932. The RFC's main function was to loan money to failing banks, railroads, insurance companies, and other big businesses. The intention was to ensure that these institutions remained intact and did not have to dissolve. That would, lawmakers hoped, create jobs and maintain existing ones, thereby helping the economy. "I want to break the ice by lending to industry so that somebody will begin to spend in a big way,"[31] Hoover's treasury secretary Ogden Mills said in 1932. The RFC did save many businesses and was also helpful when it began loaning money to individual states in late 1932. This was not enough by itself, however, to significantly improve the devastated economy.

Industrial Destruction

In fact, the combined efforts of the Hoover administration to fight the Depression failed. Month by month, year by year, the country sank deeper and deeper into a financial pit. By 1933, more than 9,000 banks in the United States had failed and closed their doors. Reports estimate that these bank failures accounted for the loss of $140 billion for regular American citizens. Because depositors had no insurance to back up their money, millions of Americans lost their entire life savings in less than a day. With millions of people losing their jobs, their savings, or both, homelessness rose sharply in the early years of the Depression.

American business and manufacturing losses during Hoover's term were also staggering. More than 26,000 businesses failed in 1930, and more than 28,000 went under the year after. By 1932, the nation's volume of manufacturing was only 54 percent of what it had been before the 1929 market crash. The struggles of the rail industry are just one example of a previously lucrative business suffering at the hands of the Depression. Going into the 1930s, railroads were still the most popular method of travel and shipping in America. As a result, large train corporations employed thousands of people. When the Depression hit, however, running a rail line became less profitable. People could not even afford food, let alone travel, and for most of the Great Depression, railroad companies were not profitable at all. An estimated one-third of America's rail companies went bankrupt in the 1930s. Tens of thousands of employees, who believed they had a stable job in a successful industry, were laid off. Because of the banking failures, this

Many railroad companies were forced to shut down in the face of the Great Depression. Hundreds of railcars were abandoned for years. The homeless often used them for shelter.

left them with no money at all.

Indeed, hundreds of thousands of families lost their homes during Hoover's years in office. All across America, the homeless gathered together and built small towns, where everyone lived in a hand-built shack in terrible conditions. Because so many people blamed his administration for the crisis, or at least for its failure to stop it, these areas, where homeless people collected and lived, became known as "Hoovervilles." In 1932, the journalist Charles Walker discovered such a place at the town waste dump in Youngstown, Ohio. "The inhabitants," he wrote, "were not … even hoboes … They were men without jobs. Life [for them] is sustained by begging, eating at the city soup kitchens, or earning a quarter by polishing an automobile."[32]

Protesting Unemployment

Motivated by the worsening economic conditions in the country, some people staged public demonstrations to show the government their anger and frustration. Thousands of marches and rallies took place across the country during the

Hoover years. These protests were sometimes broken up by force. In New York City, for instance, a large crowd was broken up by policemen using violent methods. Demonstrations and protests were similarly broken up in Detroit, Cleveland, and Boston.

The most notorious use of violence in the face of demonstrators came just a few years after the onset of the Depression. During the summer of 1932, around 15,000 World War I veterans marched on Washington, D.C., to demand that the government pay them bonus money that they had been promised but had not yet received. These men camped out near the Capitol in tents and makeshift shelters, waiting for Congress or the president to act. This group was commonly called the "Bonus Army," because they were fighting for their bonus. Most of the protestors needed that bonus money to survive. Though a large number of people made up the Bonus Army, its leader, Walter Waters, was able to keep their demonstration largely peaceful. After Congress voted down a bill that would have allowed them to collect their bonuses, most of the protestors went home. The few thousand who remained

Thousands of Americans showed up to protests such as this one, demanding that someone help the unemployed, poor, and hungry.

demonstrated more aggressively, and they soon had to deal with the real army. Soldiers drove the veterans away with tear gas and then set fire to their shelters. The crackdown wounded and killed several protestors and police officers.

These violent government reactions to discontent did not improve the national mood, and the spreading public opinion was that Hoover and his administration had to go. Historically, it is clear that the president did not cause the Depression. The unwise economic practices of the 1920s are the primary culprit. However, in spite of his good intentions, a bad situation grew worse on Hoover's watch.

Many people at the time ended up blaming Hoover for the entire crisis. One woman complained, "People are starving because of Herbert Hoover. My mother was out of work because of [him]. Men were killing themselves because of [him], and their fatherless children were being packed away to orphanages."[33]

Indeed, few Americans seemed to have fallen so far from grace as Hoover had. While he was still a popular politician in 1928, one couple had proudly named their baby Herbert Hoover Jones. Four years later, the disappointed and furious parents went to court to have the child officially renamed Franklin D. Roosevelt Jones. The boy's new namesake had just been elected president after Hoover's term ended in 1932, and he promised that he would end the country's economic nightmare. Hopes for a new beginning were high across the nation. Remembering the disaster of Hoover, beneath the surface lurked a question that was still the cause of national unrest: Could the new president deliver on his promises?

Chapter Three

A NEW LEADER

As President Herbert Hoover's administration failed to do much to improve the disastrous economic and social effects of the Great Depression, his political party—he was a Republican—was worried about the next presidential election. After all, Hoover was widely hated throughout the country for his ineffective policies, millions of people lost their jobs and savings on his watch, and the country was in the midst of its worst economic disaster ever. Maybe even worse than any of that, there were no signs that things were going to get better. People were losing faith in the Republican Party, and millions of Republicans were thinking that the Democrats might have some more, and better, answers. In the presidential election of 1932, Democrats worked hard to get their candidate elected.

The Hoover administration's economic failures led many American Democrats to think that the presidency was in a vulnerable position. It had been historically difficult to get elected over a president who was currently in office, but Franklin Delano Roosevelt, the Democratic Party's nominee, believed he could win. When the Democratic National Convention selected him in July 1932, he appealed to all citizens of the United States. He knew that the most important issue in America was fixing the economy, and he pledged to focus almost entirely on doing so. In his acceptance speech, he said,

> *My program ... is based upon this simple moral principle: the welfare and the soundness of a Nation depend [most] upon what the great mass of the people wish and need; and second, whether or not they are getting it.*

Franklin Delano Roosevelt, shown here in a portrait from 1944, was elected on his promise to end the Great Depression. He attempted to do so with his New Deal programs.

What do the people of America want more than anything else? To my mind, they want two things: work, with all the moral and spiritual values that go with it; and with work, a reasonable measure of security—security for themselves and for their wives and children ... I pledge you, I pledge myself, to a new deal for the American people. Let us all here assembled constitute ourselves prophets of a new order of competence and of courage. This is more than a political campaign; it is a call to arms. Give me your help, not to win votes alone, but to win in this crusade to restore America to its own people.[34]

Roosevelt had definite ideas for a path to financial recovery, and his political track record (He was the highly successful governor of New York from 1928 to 1932.) was positive. On Election Day in 1932, he won the presidency by a wide margin. He quickly started instituting new programs, policies, and reforms, which became known as his New Deal programs. His most important task as president was to get the economy out of the financial gutter it had been stuck in for three years.

The first three months of his term were immediately successful in stimulating the economy. This time period is now called "The Hundred Days," during which Roosevelt's long-term economic recovery plan started to take hold. It has been noted,

[Roosevelt] built a bond between himself and the public—doing much to shape the image of the President as the caretaker of the American people. Under FDR's leadership, the President's duties grew to encompass not only those of the chief executive—as implementer of policy—but also chief legislator—as drafter of policy.[35]

Out with Hoover, in with Roosevelt

Part of the reason that Roosevelt was able to make so many significant changes was that he was a skilled leader, speaker, and communicator with many years of political experience. The man whom most Americans came to call FDR was born into a wealthy family in New York's Hudson River valley. From an early age, he lived a life of privilege, and he was able to attend excellent private schools, including Harvard University. Roosevelt was also a 5th cousin of the 26th president, Theodore Roosevelt, who was in office from 1901 to 1909. Theodore "Teddy" Roosevelt is remembered as a great political reformer, and he was one of FDR's political heroes.

Franklin Roosevelt had a strong desire to use his personal gifts and privileged position to serve the public. He served as a New York State senator from 1911 to 1913, and he was an assistant

President Roosevelt was an extremely talented speaker. Shown here is a crowd that turned out to hear him give a speech in Cleveland, Ohio.

secretary of the U.S. Navy during World War I. Not long after the war, Roosevelt contracted the terrible disease polio and lost the use of his legs. Regardless, in an impressive display of courage and determination, he reentered politics, serving as governor of New York during Hoover's presidential term. His policies during this time won him respect across New York.

Many Americans thought that Roosevelt was the most appealing candidate to represent the Democratic Party in the 1932 presidential election, and he won the party's nomination. Running against Hoover, he consistently used the awful economic and social conditions of the Depression to

"A New Deal Was Absolutely Inevitable"

Franklin Roosevelt and his advisers believed that the New Deal represented a revolutionary social and economic change in the United States. This revolution, as written in 1935 by one of the chief administrators of the New Deal, Rex Tugwell, had the benefit of being peaceful and orderly:

> *A new deal was absolutely inevitable. People will submit to [a lack of basic necessities] and will even starve peaceably, if they realize that [a real lack] exists, but no man … will starve in the presence of abundance. The possibility of revolution, whether peaceful or violent, against any system which denies the visible means of life to those who have produced those means, will always be with us. Therefore, the only choice before the American people … was whether their revolution should follow the course of violence and destruction or should express itself in orderly, legal channels. The answer was given in November 1932, when the American people gave to President Roosevelt a peaceful [direction] to attempt to devise a better means of distributing the national income than had previously existed.*[1]

1. Rex Tugwell, "America Takes Hold of its Destiny," quoted in William Dudley, ed., *The Great Depression: Opposing Viewpoints*. San Diego, CA: Greenhaven Press, 1994, pp. 113–114.

campaign against the Republicans. The government needed to do more to alleviate the crisis, Roosevelt argued, and to repair the broken economy. He reached out to the poor and jobless, members of organized labor unions, racial minorities, and city dwellers, trying to forge a widespread and diverse voter base who would support and elect him.

This strategy worked phenomenally. In November 1932, Roosevelt won by a landslide, getting 472 electoral votes to Hoover's 59. The Democrats also secured a majority control of both houses of Congress, winning the House 310 to 117 and the Senate 60 to 35. Roosevelt's administration took these signs as a message from the American people: The new president needed to do anything and everything to end the Depression.

Restoring a Nation's Confidence

Roosevelt hinted at the nature and scope of this attack in his inaugural address, delivered on March 4, 1933. This speech was remarkable for a number of reasons, especially for its time. Rather than tell everyone in America that he could immediately solve every economic issue, he said that it was going to be a long, difficult path to recovery. Moreover, he said before the United States could enact political and economic change, its people must adopt a major attitude change. They must face and conquer the anxious state of fear that currently gripped the country. His address compared the country to an army that had fallen into disrepair—but he also offered a way out of their terrible condition. His advice was:

> *If we are to go forward, we must move as a trained and loyal army, willing to sacrifice for the good of a common discipline, because without such discipline no progress can be made, no leadership becomes effective. We are, I know, ready and willing to submit our lives and our property to such discipline because it makes possible a leadership which aims at the larger good ... I assume unhesitatingly the leadership of this great army of our people dedicated to a disciplined attack upon our common problems.*[36]

Reactions to Roosevelt's speech were universally favorable. After years of what many perceived as governmental inaction, a mood of active optimism began to spread across the nation. The American humorist and political commentator Will Rogers captured that mood when he stated,

> *America hasn't been so happy in three years as they are today. No money, no banks, no work, no nothing, but they know they got a man in there who is wise to Congress, wise to our big bankers, and wise to our so-called big men. The whole country is with him even if what he does is wrong. They are with him, just so he does something. If he burned down the Capitol we would cheer and say, "Well, we at least got a fire started, anyhow."*[37]

Roosevelt and his advisers knew that they had a lot of work to do to earn the people's trust. However, the truth was that the country's economic crisis was so huge and serious that no one, not even the finest economists of the time, knew how to begin fixing it. As a result, the new administration launched a bold, broad attack on the Depression. Leaders initiated an array of programs, most of them experimentally, hoping that at least some would work. This was an exact opposite to Hoover's conservative approach, in which government played a minimal role. Roosevelt assigned the federal government the chief role in the recovery.

Through Roosevelt's New Deal programs, millions of homeless and unemployed Americans tried to get back on their feet.

A Necessary Pause

The first major move Roosevelt's government made was an attempt to stabilize the value of U.S. currency, which had been declining. This would help restore confidence in America's banks. On March 6, 1933, not even two days after he had taken office, the president called a special session of Congress. Standing before the legislators, he called for a national bank holiday. This meant that all the nation's banks would close down until March 10, 1933, and allow accountants from the U.S. Treasury to inspect their records and transactions. This would reveal which banks were most in need of emergency government aid. Then, only the banks whose finances were sound enough would be allowed to reopen.

Though this was a daring and unprecedented move, most congressmen, senators, and bankers felt it was

A Fireside Chat

In his first radio broadcast on March 12, 1933, President Roosevelt tried to both explain to the American people the reasons for the bank holiday and reassure them that it would help the national economy:

> *First of all, let me state the simple fact that when you deposit money in a bank, the bank does not put the money into a safe deposit vault. It invests your money in many different … kinds of loans. In other words, the bank puts your money to work to keep the wheels of industry and of agriculture turning around … Because of undermined confidence on the part of the public, there was a general rush by a large portion of our population to turn bank deposits into currency or gold—a rush so great that the soundest banks couldn't get enough currency to meet the demand … [So] I issued the proclamation providing for the national bank holiday … [This] is affording us the opportunity to supply the currency necessary to meet the situation. Remember that no sound bank is a dollar worse off than it was when it closed its doors last week.*[1]

1. Quoted in Franklin Delano Roosevelt, "First Fireside Chat: Delivered 12 March 1933, Washington D.C.," American Rhetoric. www.americanrhetoric.com/speeches/fdrfirstfiresidechat.html.

necessary. Therefore, they passed the bank holiday bill: The House of Representatives swiftly approved it, and a few hours later, the Senate passed it nearly unanimously. Only seven hours after submitting the bill to Congress, Roosevelt signed it into law. It was the fastest passage of a piece of federal legislation in U.S. history.

Roosevelt realized that national legislators were not the only people whose support was needed to make the bank holiday a success. It was important for ordinary citizens, on whose financial deposits banks depended, to understand what was happening. To explain his strategy, on March 12, 1933, the president held his first "fireside chat." Repeated throughout his presidency, fireside chats were radio addresses in which he outlined national problems and challenges and explained or defended government policies. "[A] question you will ask is this," he stated in the first broadcast:

Roosevelt's fireside chats were revolutionary. He addressed the concerns of the common American citizen, and many people appreciated his transparency.

> *Why are all the banks not to be reopened at the same time? The answer is simple and I know you will understand it: Your Government does not intend that the history of the past few years shall be repeated. We do not want and will not have another epidemic of bank failures.*
>
> *As a result, we start tomorrow, Monday, with the opening of the banks ... which on first examination by the Treasury, have already been found to be all right ... [Later, banks] all through the country will resume business ... Please let me make it clear to you that if your bank does not open the first day you are by no means justified in believing it will not open.*[38]

The broadcast helped millions of Americans understand and benefit from the sweeping bank closures and reopenings. The new administration quickly ended the worst of the national banking crisis and restored public confidence in the country's banks. About a week after declaring the bank holiday, Roosevelt wrote to an old friend, "We seem to be off to a good start and I hope to get through some important legislation while the feeling of the country is so friendly."[39]

The Start of a New Deal

Roosevelt was not content to simply pass "some" legislation, however. He wanted to completely reorganize and revolutionize the federal government. To do so, he pushed through a startling amount of bills and policies. The number and magnitude of the federal programs he introduced in his first hundred days in office easily exceeded what some presidents had accomplished in their entire four-year terms. In March 1933, the same month in which he declared the bank holiday, Roosevelt called for the creation of a major new aid program.

This organization was named the Civilian Conservation Corps (CCC). Run by the military, its primary function was to provide work for the hundreds of thousands of young men who did not have work. They would be employed to plant trees, fight forest fires, and dig ditches. Though this was not skilled labor, the CCC gave more than 3 million young men a job from 1933 to 1942. This not only reduced the unemployment rate, but also increased the amount of money being spent by civilians in the economy. Most importantly, the program allowed the young men who worked for it to survive. It was far from the only government-sponsored program in the 1930s to do so.

The Agricultural Adjustment Administration (AAA), formed in May 1933, was a bold and controversial piece of legislation. Its purpose was to increase the profits of poor farmers by having them reduce the amount of grain, corn, rice, livestock, and other items they produced. The hope was that, as these commodities became less common, they would be worth more. This would lead to a price increase for agricultural goods, and farmers' wages would increase as well.

Initial reactions to the AAA were mixed. Economists saw the wisdom of the plan, and farmers were happy to make more money. Many ordinary Americans, however, objected to the idea of producing less food at a time when many people were starving. They especially disliked it when AAA officials ordered that millions of farm animals be slaughtered and thousands of acres of cotton be destroyed, which would help raise prices and profits for farmers. As McElvaine wrote,

> *What sense did it make to destroy food in a nation where millions were hungry and a world where hundreds of millions were starving? Very little, perhaps, but no less than it did*

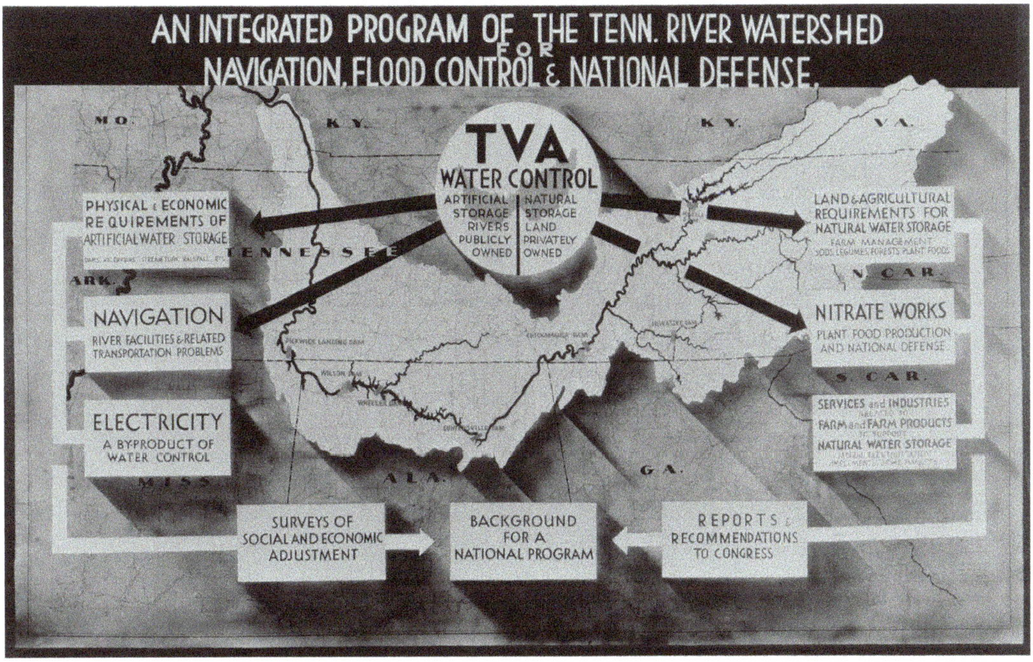

This map from around 1940 shows the plan for the Tennessee Valley Authority, which still operates today.

> *to have such poverty and want in the midst of abundance ... The AAA concept of limiting production was no more [illogical] than the economic system itself, which found no way to bring together idle [unused] workers and idle factories or hungry people and unsold crops.*[40]

The Hundred Days also created the Federal Emergency Relief Administration (FERA), organized in May 1933. Roosevelt appointed his friend and adviser, Harry Hopkins, as director of this important new agency. FERA was designed to reduce adult unemployment. It disbursed funds to individual states, allowing them to establish and run local work projects. After just two years, FERA was disbanded and replaced with the Works Progress Administration (WPA), but in that time, it provided jobs to more than 20 million Americans who had been out of work.

Still another of Roosevelt's daring and effective programs was the Tennessee Valley Authority (TVA), also created in May 1933. One of the largest construction projects in world history, it aimed to construct a series of huge dams in the Tennessee River Valley. The structures, Roosevelt claimed, would give millions of Americans cheap electricity, help control damaging

Helping the New Deal

Harry Hopkins, one of the major architects of the New Deal and one of Roosevelt's trusted advisers, was born in Iowa in 1890. As a young man, he served in various social work and relief organizations, including the American Red Cross, and became an advocate for child welfare. While Roosevelt was still governor, he hired Hopkins to run New York's relief organization in the Depression's early years. Now the president, in March 1933, Roosevelt made Hopkins director of the Federal Emergency Relief Administration (FERA). Later, Hopkins ran the Civil Works Administration (CWA) and founded the Works Progress Administration (WPA). Hopkins truly believed in the objectives of the New Deal, and by 1938, he had spent more than $8.5 billion on unemployment relief efforts. He died on January 29, 1946.

floods that occurred almost every year in the area, and provide years of work for tens of thousands of people. "This is the story of a great change," one of the TVA's directors, David Lilienthal, later said, describing how much the project meant to citizens living along the Tennessee River. He continued,

> *It is a tale of a wandering and inconstant river [that became] a chain of broad and lovely lakes which people enjoy, and on which they can depend, in all seasons ... It is a story of how waters once wasted and destructive have been controlled and now work, night and day, creating electric energy to lighten the burden of human [labor]. Here is a tale of fields grown ... vigorous with new fertility ... of forests ... now protected and refreshed.*[41]

The TVA was an overwhelming success. It supplied inexpensive power to millions of Americans, provided long-term jobs for thousands of people, and improved natural conservation efforts in the region.

Waiting for Success

Though they are the most well known, the CCC, AAA, FERA, and TVA were not the only important programs the Roosevelt administration introduced in the historic Hundred Days. Some of the others included the Economy Act, which was intended to reduce the size of the federal government; the Truth-in-Securities Act, which was organized to reform the stock market and make future crashes less likely; and the Home Owners Loan Act, which helped people of lower incomes obtain mortgages so that they could buy a home.

As these comprehensive programs started to roll out, the American people started to regain confidence in the future. The general view was that even if some of these programs did not work, at least the government was making a real effort to turn things around. Though some conservative observers criticized the growing role of the government, most people were simply happy to have food and a home. One of Roosevelt's advisers, Raymond Moley, later recalled, "During the [Hundred Days] Congress, people didn't know what was going on ... They knew something was happening, something good for them. They began investing and working and hoping again."[42]

Moreover, the American people were not the only ones closely watching the way Roosevelt was fighting the Depression. Many other countries were experiencing the same dramatic financial slump. They hoped that America's ongoing economic and political experiments would be successful—if they were, their effects would ripple outward and help everyone. Noted British politician Winston Churchill summed it up well: "The courage, the power and the scale [of Roosevelt's effort]," he said, "must enlist the ardent sympathy of every country, and his success could not fail to lift the whole world forward into ... [a] more [happy] age."[43]

Chapter Four

PROGRAMS FOR RECOVERY

Around the world, and especially within the United States itself, people were amazed at the number, extent, and success of President Roosevelt's Hundred Days programs. Though the American economy was still far from restored, the New Deal initiatives and legislation were helping it find its way back to prosperity. Moreover, the programs instituted during the Hundred Days were far from the only successful governmental actions taken by Roosevelt's administration against the Great Depression. He was elected president a total of four times, and he never stopped trying to improve the country.

Though Roosevelt himself was an intelligent, creative, and qualified individual, his presidential terms were supported by a group of men nicknamed the "Brain Trust" by the journalist John F. Kieran. This term was widespread immediately, and most Americans associated FDR's success with the members of the Brain Trust. The most prominent members of this group were Rexford Tugwell, Adolf Berle Jr., and Raymond Moley, all three of whom were professors at Columbia University, one of the top schools in the country. They advised Roosevelt on a range of political fields—from economic issues to social problems.

Critics of the Brain Trust accused its members of being idealistic, irresponsible spenders and of being disconnected from the problems they were trying to solve. Though their programs were certainly not all successful, they believed in the philosophy that got FDR elected: Try everything until something works. The programs and institutions they suggested were often unique and bold ways of addressing the nation's massive

Rexford Tugwell (left) was a prominent member of FDR's (middle) Brain Trust. He was an expert economist, and he advised the president about how to end the Great Depression.

economic problems. Any new idea that seemed promising was given a chance to succeed. The New Deal era was a time of experimentation; because no one had ever seen an economic crisis similar to the Depression, the Brain Trust and FDR believed that they needed solutions that had never been seen before, either.

Risky Programs

The new programs created by FDR's administration ranged from resounding successes to mediocre failures. None of his initiatives were truly catastrophic, and many were extraordinarily helpful for millions of Americans. Roosevelt knew he was taking a political risk by creating unique programs, but that was part of his strategy. Gardiner C. Means, who held high positions in several New Deal agencies, later remembered,

> *It was ... experimentation that made the New Deal what it was. A hundred years from now, when historians look back on it, they will*

A Powerful President

A huge majority of Americans supported the New Deal for so long because they truly believed in President Roosevelt. Nearly everyone perceived him as a larger-than-life character who, though certainly not perfect, was working hard for the nation's greater good. One of his biographers summed up his revolutionary presidential tenure:

> *Under FDR's energetic leadership the government became an active participant in the economic life of the nation. More important, he restored the country's confidence. Roosevelt revolutionized the art of political campaigning, revitalized the Democratic party, and created a new national majority that included those previously cast aside. His fireside chats brought the presidency to every living room in America.*[1]

1. Jean Edward Smith, *FDR*. New York, NY: Random House, 2007, p. ix.

> *say a big corner was turned. People agreed that old things didn't work. What ran through the whole New Deal was finding a way to make things work … We had meetings that would run into the early morning. A dozen of us sitting around a table, thrashing out problems … There was no question in our minds that we were saving the country.*[44]

The approach of remaking the nation through trial and error was a big part of the spirit of the New Deal and of the times. It certainly worked effectively to lower unemployment and stimulate the economy, but it was nonetheless a major gamble. "Everybody was searching for ideas," a New Deal economist later wrote,

> *[T]here was a search, a sense of values [that] would make a difference in the lives of people … There were weaknesses [in the New Deal], but the point is if you wanted to get jobs for people in a hurry … you had to find new [government leaders] with the spirit, with the drive.*[45]

FDR's grand experiment in fighting the Depression, reorganizing the economy, and changing society paid off, both for him and the country. He was able to lead the United States through the Great Depression and through most of World War II. Some of his programs, however, have been criticized, and conservative Republicans believed that the government was getting too big. FDR was open-minded, but some critics believed that he was too willing to try new things:

> *Many of his programs were turned on and off, started and stopped … Planning had not been done … I was enthusiastic when Roosevelt came in … I voted for him his first term and his second, [but] I became terribly disenchanted.*
>
> *He was a dramatic leader. He had charm, personality, poise and so on. He could inspire people. But to me, he lacked the [perseverance] to carry a program through.*[46]

Assisting Everyone

Critiques of FDR's ability to complete his big ideas were both right and wrong. It is true that a number of Roosevelt's New Deal programs did close down after only a few years of operation. However, some lasted for more than decade, and some were so enormously successful that as of 2017, they are still in operation. One example of this is the Tennessee Valley Authority, which still provides power to millions of Americans. Another is Social Security, which is one of the most prominent social fixtures in the country.

The goal of the Social Security Act, implemented in August 1935, was to help citizens who are in particular need because of old age, job loss, or some kind of disability. Both employers and working people contribute to a special Social Security fund, and the Social Security Administration then distributes the money to people who are older than 65, temporarily unemployed, or too sick to work. When signing the act into law, Roosevelt said,

> *We can never insure one hundred percent of the population against one hundred percent of [life's] hazards, but we have tried to frame a law which will give some measure of protection to the average citizen and to his family against the loss of a job and against poverty ridden old age.*[47]

Just as it is a widely debated political topic today, it was a controversial initiative when Roosevelt and his advisers proposed it. Many people, especially conservatives, argued against it, because it entailed the government giving people money they had not directly earned. They worried that this was potentially harmful because it could promote laziness, or reward people for not working. Conservative Republican senator Daniel O. Hastings of Delaware, for

Social Security, a program which is still in place as of 2017, was founded in 1935. This stamp was created to celebrate its 50th anniversary in 1985.

example, argued that Social Security would make Americans lazy, wasteful, and cowardly. "I fear it may end the progress of a great country," he said, and "discourage and defeat the American trait of thrift. It will go a long way toward destroying American initiative and courage."[48] James L. Donnelly, a former spokesman for the Illinois Manufacturers' Association, agreed. He warned that Social Security would undermine American life and American values "by destroying initiative, discouraging thrift, and stifling individual responsibility."[49]

Roosevelt and the many Americans who supported the idea of Social Security countered by pointing out that the new system did not simply give people free money. Every person who ever did any sort of work would pay a little into the system. Therefore, they would contribute to their own retirement. Moreover, economists argued that the program was a wise way to help guard against future depressions and mass poverty. As Frances Perkins, U.S. secretary of labor under FDR, put it,

> *Our social security program will be a vital force working against the*

Activist and Administrator

Harold L. Ickes was one of the leading U.S. government officials in the 1930s and 1940s, and he was a major contributor to the New Deal during the Depression era. Born in Pennsylvania in 1874, he was a social activist and lawyer. In his early life, he provided legal representation for clients suing for civil liberties, oftentimes at no charge. Soon, he became a Republican political operative, supporting the policies of FDR's cousin, President Theodore Roosevelt. In 1933, Franklin Roosevelt, a Democrat who wanted a Republican in his cabinet for the sake of balance, asked Ickes to serve as secretary of the interior. In this position, he is most remembered for defending natural resources against corporate exploitation. Ickes also served as director of the Public Works Administration (PWA), where he disbursed billions of dollars to give unemployed Americans jobs. Ickes was a powerful champion of civil liberties and civil rights. He also openly criticized the government's internment of Japanese Americans during World War II. Ickes resigned from the government early in 1946 after arguing with President Harry Truman. He died in Washington, D.C., in 1952.

Harold Ickes was one of President Roosevelt's top advisers. He was highly progressive, and he advocated for racial and social equality.

recurrence of severe depressions in the future. We can, as the principle of sustained purchasing power in hard times makes itself felt in every shop, store and mill, grow old without being haunted by the [threat] of a poverty-ridden old age or of being a burden on our children ... The American people want such security as the law provides. It will make this great Republic a better and a happier place in which to live—for us, our children, and our children's children.[50]

Economists are still debating the positive and negative aspects of the Social Security Act. Though some prominent members of government have rigorously supported it, some observers have argued that it should be narrowed or completely disbanded. What it has unquestionably done, however, is provide a stable income for millions of Americans who cannot work.

Finally, Employment

Some of the most successful New Deal initiatives were created with the primary goal of putting the millions of unemployed Americans back to work. In this regard, the CCC was a hallmark program. A poll taken by Gallup, a data collection and analysis corporation, in 1936 found that 82 percent of Americans were strongly in favor of the CCC because it found decent-paying work for millions of young men. The program lasted 9 years and at its height, employed 500,000 men simultaneously. Though it closed down in 1942, it likely would have remained active had the United States not entered World War II. After the country began fighting, most of the young men who would have found jobs through the CCC joined the military instead.

A large portion of other Americans managed to find employment through Roosevelt's PWA. This popular program was headed by the secretary of the interior, Harold L. Ickes. Known for his honesty, organizational skills, and work ethic, Ickes was one of leading figures of the New Deal and a major player in the U.S. government from 1933 to 1946. Under his guidance, the PWA struck deals with private contractors to construct buildings, highways, and other public works projects. Its goal was to both employ as many citizens as possible and improve the infrastructure of the country.

The scope of the PWA's accomplishments was huge. Between 1933 and 1939, it spent $4 billion to employ Americans to build a total of more than 34,000 streets, highways, schools, dams, airports, hospitals, sewage systems, tunnels, and warships. Of these projects, a huge portion were schools and roads of various types. Among the best-known public works the agency created are New York City's Lincoln Tunnel, Washington State's Grand Coulee Dam, and the Overseas Highway connecting Key West, Florida, to

Writing History

Part of the Works Progress Administration (WPA), the Federal Writers' Project (FWP) was created in 1935 to help unemployed writers, editors, and other scholarly professionals find work. Its first director was a successful theatrical producer named Henry Alsberg. Over the course of several years, the FWP employed more than 6,600 writers, editors, historians, art critics, archaeologists, and others, each of whom earned a salary of roughly $20 per week. Their job was to compile or create local histories, oral histories, children's books, and other written documents that recorded and promoted American lifestyles and values.

The agency's best-known products were 48 state guides published as part of the *American Guide* series. Each book in the series provided a history of the state and descriptions of each of its cities and towns. Among the writers who worked in the FWP were Studs Terkel, who later became famous for his oral history of the Depression era; black novelist Richard Wright; and noted author Zora Neale Hurston. Other writers, such as John Steinbeck, famous for his novels *The Grapes of Wrath* and *Of Mice and Men*, were deeply inspired by the *American Guide* series of books produced by the FWP.

the U.S. mainland.

Even more widespread than the PWA was another New Deal program designed to put people to work: the WPA. Created in 1935, the WPA was headed by Harry Hopkins, who also directed the Federal Emergency Relief Administration. The WPA was the single largest New Deal program by a significant margin. From 1935 to 1943, 8.5 million Americans in a wide range of professions were employed by the WPA. Like the other New Deal initiatives, the WPA built roads, bridges, and airport runways, which were critical pieces of infrastructure. The WPA also erected libraries, city halls, and parks, and devoted 7 percent of its budget to funding arts-related projects. Among the sub-programs of the WPA were the Federal Writers' Project, the Federal Theatre Project, and the Federal Music Project. These and other similar programs helped America's artists and authors find an outlet for their creative talents. They were a vital part of keeping the rich culture of the country alive through the difficult Depression years.

Industrial Legislation

Most of these large-scale employment programs implemented during the New Deal were designed to create new jobs, which would allow the millions of unemployed Americans to earn money. Some of this money would be spent, and this would stimulate the depressed economy. Millions of Americans had been fortunate enough to keep their jobs in existing industries and businesses, but many others, who had specific skills in these industries, had recently been laid off. Large numbers of big employers had cut back, partly because their businesses were disorganized, not working to capacity, taking advantage of their workers, or any combination of these factors.

In an effort to make American industry more efficient and fair, which would lead to expansion and the hiring of more people, the Roosevelt administration proposed the National Industrial Recovery Act (NIRA). Congress passed it in 1933, and its centerpiece became the National Recovery Administration (NRA), headed by Hugh S. Johnson, who was a retired military general and a member of FDR's Brain Trust. The NRA was designed to help factories and other large businesses plan for the future; to restore competition in the market, which had diminished along with the suffering economy; to regulate prices so that industries could not unfairly overcharge consumers; to set the number of hours employees could work each week, which would reduce exploitation of the workers; and to eliminate child labor. McElvaine described the NRA's major goals and how Johnson expected to accomplish them:

> *The idea behind the NRA, quite simply, was to introduce rational planning into what had been a chaotic economic system. By providing balance to the economy, the NRA, it was hoped, would restore employment and prosperity … Under the NRA, each industry in the country would draw up a code of practices that would be acceptable. These would cover wages, working conditions, and … prices and production … In his second fireside chat, Franklin Roosevelt called the NRA "a partnership in planning" between business and government.*[51]

The goals set by the NRA were broad, were diverse, and affected tens of millions of employers and employees across all levels of society. Collecting reliable data from hundreds of thousands of businesses across the country was a monumental undertaking. It is unclear how successful each aspect of the program was and how much it actually helped the economy. The consensus of historians is that even though the NRA did not single-handedly lift the country out the Depression in the 1930s, it was a crucial component of the country's long-term economic stability. "The NRA was one of most successful things the New Deal did," Gardiner Means pointed out,

> *[W]hen it was created, American business was completely demoralized. Violent price-cutting and wage-cutting [were widespread and] nobody could make any plans for tomorrow … The NRA changed the attitudes of business and the public. It revived belief that something [positive] could be done.*[52]

McElvaine added that Hugh Johnson "made no attempt to use his authority to dictate codes to businessmen. Instead, he negotiated with them."[53] This was an important step for the federal government: The NRA taught politicians that it was possible for cooperation between government and business to exist.

Far from Perfection

Even if the NRA was not an immediate success, it achieved far more than some other New Deal ventures. An experiment as bold, widespread, and unique as the New Deal was bound to produce at least a few failed initiatives. One of the most notable and controversial examples was the Civil Works Administration (CWA). Initiated in October 1933, the CWA was supposed to put millions of people to work immediately. However, it has been noted,

> *At first, it seemed to be on the right track. By January 1934, the CWA had more than 4.2 million people on its employment rolls. But the problem with the program was that it was too unstructured. A lot of people were receiving federal money for questionable or trivial endeavors—raking leaves, for example. And Roosevelt himself saw that the potential existed for creating a class of 'reliefers' who might become [forever] dependent on the government.*[54]

This was in contrast to the CCC and later the PWA and WPA, which created more substantial, sustainable, and significant jobs. Accordingly, FDR admitted that the CWA was not going to be a success, and it was discontinued in 1934, barely a year after its creation.

Another unwise political strategy to arise from FDR's administration was its attempt to change the Supreme Court. Toward the end of his first term, the high court began declaring some of his progressive programs illegal or unconstitutional. Among these outlawed programs were the NRA in 1935 and AAA in 1936. The president and most of his advisers thought that these decisions were the result of too many old, conservative judges on the court—men born in the middle of the 1800s who were old-fashioned and suspicious of new and liberal ideas. In his ninth fireside chat, broadcast on March 9, 1937, Roosevelt told the American people,

Despite the best efforts of Roosevelt and his Brain Trust, unemployment and poverty were still high in America. Millions of people still relied on public assistance.

In the last four years ... the [Supreme] Court has been acting not as a judicial body, but as a policy-making body ... The Court ... has improperly set itself up as a third house of the Congress—a super-legislature, as one of the justices has called it—reading into the

Constitution words and implications which are not there, and which were never intended to be there.

We have, therefore, reached the point as a nation where we must take action to save the Constitution from the Court and the Court from itself. We must find a way to take an appeal from the Supreme Court to the Constitution itself. We want a Supreme Court which will do justice under the Constitution and not over it.[55]

FDR attempted to work around the Supreme Court by introducing the Judiciary Reorganization Bill of 1937. His political opponents were quick to label it the "court-packing bill." Its main purpose was to give the president the right to appoint an extra Supreme Court justice for each existing judge who was older than 70. Each of these extra judges would be hand-picked for their loyalty to FDR and his New Deal. Considering the configuration of the Court at the time, this would have expanded it by an extra six justices, and it would have ensured that most or all

Shown here are the Supreme Court justices at the time of Roosevelt's controversial "court-packing bill." He argued that they were too old-fashioned to accept his New Deal.

of Roosevelt's programs would thereafter be deemed constitutional.

The bill raised protests from both Republicans and Democrats. Opponents worried that it would give the office of president too much authority and create an imbalance of power among the executive, legislative, and judicial bodies of government. Accordingly, the Senate rejected the idea almost immediately. "This bill [is] a needless, futile, and utterly dangerous abandonment of constitutional principle," the senators concluded. "It is a proposal without precedent and without justification. It would subjugate the courts to the will of Congress and the President and thereby destroy the independence of the judiciary."[56]

FDR lost in his attempt to restructure the Supreme Court. However, for reasons that are still debated by historians, the high court began to vote more often in his favor after his bill was defeated. As a result, most elements of the New Deal remained in place throughout FDR's presidency. The Great Depression, meanwhile, had not yet left the country, even by the mid-1930s.

Chapter Five

LIFE IN UNCERTAIN TIMES

For a huge portion of Americans during the Great Depression, the only thing available was not food, shelter, or a job—it was despair. More than 10 million people were unemployed and countless numbers of people lost their savings and went homeless. Those who did retain their jobs were often paid significantly less than they had been earning just a few years before the stock market crash of 1929. It was a bleak, uninspiring time in the United States. Even after President Roosevelt's successful New Deal programs began providing some relief, the end was still not in sight for most Americans.

Even in the terrible conditions of the Depression, families still went on living. Men and women tried to provide the best life possible for their children, even if that meant living in a crowded apartment or giving up excess spending. Many people could not even afford new clothes:

> *"Everything I own I have on my back," [one man] said. He then explained that, having no underwear, he was wearing two pairs of overalls … His shoes were so [old] that I wondered how he kept them on his feet … The women and children are even worse off than the men. When there has been any money at all, it has gone for shoes for the children.*[57]

In areas where it got cold during the winter, the situation was even more dangerous. People without proper clothing, let alone a home to shelter them, had nothing to protect them from the deadly cold. Desperate was this description of a Midwestern winter in 1932, written by an investigative reporter:

> *Last Winter the temperature went down to 40 degrees below zero and stayed there ten days, while a 60-mile*

[per hour] wind howled across the plains. And entering that kind of Winter we have between 4,000 and 5,000 human beings ... without clothing or bedding, getting just enough food to keep them from starving. No fuel. Living in houses that a prosperous farmer wouldn't put his cattle in.[58]

In America's cities, the people were not living much differently. Thousands of people were put out onto the street, and they could often not even afford to feed their families. Hundreds of thousands of people waited for hours—sometimes all day—in long, winding lines outside of soup and bread kitchens. They simply had no other way to access food with no money. Resulting from these cruel conditions, thousands of people committed suicide during the early years of the Great Depression. Those who did not take their own lives were still stuck in an endless cycle of misery and pessimism.

Given the extremely difficult times, it would be reasonable to expect that people did not spend much money on recreation. However, because there was little to be optimistic about in their real lives, people tried to entertain themselves so that they could have a break from their troubles. In the 1930s, millions of people were spending a great deal of their income on leisure activities, such as movies, radio programs, and live shows.

Jobs Wanted

One of the worst aspects of the Depression for many people was unemployment. The economy simply could not support enough jobs after the stock market crash of 1929, and there had been little improvement during Hoover's presidency. Few jobs were available before Roosevelt's New Deal programs began putting people back to work. As successful as these programs were, they did not eradicate the terrible unemployment epidemic. In 1935, for example, the unemployment rate was still a crippling 20 percent, and as late as 1940, it remained high at 14.5 percent.

The task of job-hunting, therefore, became a prominent and familiar feature of Depression life in towns and cities across the United States. In fact, huge numbers of men, who far outnumbered women as members of the workforce at the time, relentlessly searched for work, even when they knew no jobs were available. The reason for this fanatical search was ingrained in the American spirit: It was a good work ethic. Traditionally, a man was responsible for supporting his family while his wife and children maintained their home. This was at the centerpiece of 1930s lifestyles. "Americans had been brought up on the belief that meaningful work is the basis of life," McElvaine pointed out. He continued,

A widespread attitude of the unemployed early in the Depression was: "There must be something wrong with a [man] who can't get a job."

Unemployment was one of the most widespread problems during the Great Depression. Millions of men and women suddenly found themselves on the streets.

> Sure, I've lost my job, but I'm still a worthy provider. Work will turn up soon. *Every morning up before dawn, washed, shaved, and dressed as neatly as possible. To the factory gates, only to find a hundred others already there, staring blankly at the sign: NO HELP WANTED. The search then became more feverish.*[59]

Because of the harsh conditions of their unemployed lives, job-hunters began to look older and more worn out. This made it even harder for them to find work. An Oklahoma woman explained the problem in a 1934 letter to FDR's wife, Eleanor Roosevelt, "The unemployed have been so long without food-clothes-shoes-medical care-dental care-etc., [that] we look pretty bad-so when we ask for a job we don't get it. And we look and feel a little worse each day—when we ask for food, they call us bums."[60]

"Bums" was only one of many derogatory terms commonly used against unemployed men and women during the Depression. In fact, people without jobs were often the victims of prejudice by people who had been fortunate enough to keep their steady work. Typical bad names aimed at poverty-stricken men and their families were: "'thieves and lazy, immoral people,' 'no good for nothing loafers,' 'human parasites,' and 'pampered poverty rats.'"[61]

The worst part of these verbal torments was the undeniable psychological impact they carried. Most American men were used to being breadwinners—providers who worked to give their families a good life—and they did not know what it meant to be unemployed. For some, the only way out appeared to be suicide. Joseph L. Heffernan, mayor of Youngstown, Ohio, during the Depression's early years, remembered an unemployed man who came to him asking for work: "One man I had known for years stood at my desk and calmly said, 'My wife is frantic. After working at the steel mill for twenty-five years, I have lost my job, and I'm too old to get other work. If you can't do something for me, I'm going to kill myself.'"[62]

Mayor Heffernan was able to secure this particular man a job, and he did not end up taking his own life; many others were not so lucky. A mechanic living in Houston, Texas is just one example of the tragedy of the Depression's widespread unemployment. Before killing himself, he left a note that read,

> *The depression has got me [beaten]. There is no work to be had. I can't accept charity and I am too proud to appeal to my [family] or friends, and I am too honest to steal. So I see no other course. A land flowing with milk and honey and a first class mechanic can't make an honest living. I would rather take my chances with a just God than with unjust humanity.*[63]

The psychological effects of long-term unemployment were lethal. America's national suicide rate rose from 12 per 100,000 in 1929 to more than 17 per 100,000 in 1932. This was a jump of almost 50 percent. Moreover, the rate was even higher in many cities that had been hit particularly hard by the Depression.

Family Roles Change

Widespread unemployment and poverty also disrupted traditional family roles in communities all across the country. The usual status and responsibilities of men, women, and children in these families changed, sometimes dramatically. In particular, the status of the man as the primary breadwinner and head of the family diminished. Before the Depression, a man generally dominated because his job supported the family. When he could no longer provide for them, society began to experience some changes. If a man could not reliably make money, people began questioning why he was the leader of the family.

In addition, many men found themselves stuck hanging around the house. They were intruding into what had traditionally been the woman's sphere. One positive result of this trend was that many men learned to see things more from a woman's perspective. As McElvaine pointed out,

In certain respects, the Depression can be seen as having [caused] a "feminization" of American society. The self-centered, aggressive, competitive "male" ethic of the 1920s was discredited. Men who lost their jobs became dependent in ways that women had been thought to be … men in the Depression found themselves much more often in the traditional position of women … in a state of dependence … Depression victims tended to [associate with] "female" values. They sought to escape dependence not through "male," self-centered, "rugged" individualism, but through cooperation and compassion.[64]

In some families, however, men being stuck in the house all day led to negative consequences. Some couples, together all day and all night and suffering from poverty, unemployment, and hunger, were more likely to get into arguments. In some cases, a husband was unable to find work, but other members of his immediate family were able to secure a job. This could damage a man's pride and make him more likely to lash out violently at relatives. Though divorce rates during the Depression decreased, some historians claim that this is because people could not afford the legal fees of a divorce. Reports also indicate that the rate of marriage desertion (simply walking away from one's spouse) increased in the 1930s.

Even in cases where parents stayed together, children suffered as well. Parents under stress commonly passed their own worries on to their sons and daughters. During the early years of the Depression, one man from Arizona said, "Sometimes you would look at your children and wonder what would happen to them … Often you cry like a youngster; you try to do it privately, but you know the children hear you."[65]

Only a fortunate few children were able to remain in school; many others were not. Because of financial disaster, numerous towns and cities across the nation were forced to close some of their public schools. Other children had to quit school to help their parents make ends meet. Young boys worked in fields or helped repair aging and failing family vehicles. Young girls helped their mothers make or mend clothes and looked after younger siblings. Nationwide, 3 million children between the ages of 7 and 17 had left school by the 1930s. Some of them managed to find work outside the home through FDR's Civilian Conservation Corps, but many who quit school remained jobless for years.

Trying to Escape

Whether someone had a job during the Depression or not, surviving from one week to the next was life's major priority. No matter how hard things got, though, most people somehow managed to squeeze out enough time and money to have some fun whenever they could. In fact, Americans pursued a wide range of leisure and entertainment activities all throughout the 1930s. Sporting events, including baseball and football games, were widely popular. So were holiday parades and picnics, high school band concerts, community dances, county fairs, and carnivals that traveled from town to town.

In addition, by far the most popular form of entertainment in that era was going to the movies. For millions of Americans, watching films was a way to escape from the bleak reality of their lives. Moreover, nearly every town in the country had at least one small movie theater, so they were easily accessible. These places were nearly always packed; between 60 million and 70 million people—roughly 50 percent of the entire population of the United States—attended a movie at least once a week during the 1930s. The main reason that so many people could afford it was that tickets were inexpensive. On average, admission cost just 10 to 20 cents for adults and 5 to 10 cents for children. Moviegoers got

Though the football played in the 1930s was not quite the same as modern football, it was a popular attraction. Admission was relatively inexpensive, and a good game could entertain the whole family for hours.

a lot for their money, as well; included in the single ticket price, most theaters ran two full-length movies, one or two shorter cartoons, and a short newsreel summarizing the national and world events of the past week.

Depression-era Americans were also drawn to movie theaters by the specific subject matter of films. For the most part, films set in reality or depicting life realistically were not popular in the 1930s. These films reminded people of the harsh world they had to return to after leaving the theater, which defeated the entire purpose of attending a movie. Instead, most moviegoers preferred to be transported into over-the-top or fantasy worlds. Musicals, such as *42nd Street* (1933) and *The Gold Diggers of 1935* (1935), were widely popular, as well as Westerns. The most popular Western of the decade was *Stagecoach* (1939), directed by John Ford and starring John Wayne, who is remembered as one of the most famous actors of all time.

Moviegoers also enjoyed seeing gangster films, such as *Little Caesar* (1931); horror films, such as *Frankenstein* (1931); silly comedies, such as *Bringing Up Baby* (1938); and historical or fantasy epics, such as *Gone With the Wind* (1939) and *The Wizard of Oz* (1939). Because the movie industry was relatively prosperous during the Depression, movie quality generally increased. Some films released in the 1930s are among the most highly regarded movies of all time.

John Wayne was one of the lead actors in Stagecoach. *The film was widely popular, and Wayne would go on to act in dozens of blockbuster movies.*

Optimism Against Adversity

Depression-era Americans went to see *Gone with the Wind*, set during the American Civil War, in huge numbers in 1939. So many people went, in fact, that it was one of the most popular and successful films of all time. Part of the appeal to 1930s audiences was the onscreen dilemma of the main character, Scarlet O'Hara (played by Vivien Leigh). Originally a rich, spoiled woman from the South, she lost everything in the Civil War, which forced her to start over with only her wits and courage to guide her. This struggle was closely related to the experiences of many Americans in the 1930s. Scarlet's famous final line, "After all, tomorrow is another day,"[1] was a fitting message of hope to end a decade during which so many Americans had concluded that all hope was lost.

1. Sidney Howard, *Gone with the Wind*, directed by Victor Fleming, aired 1939 (Burbank, CA: Warner Home Video, 2009), DVD.

Listening, Gambling, and Dancing

Another advantage of going to the movies in the Depression era was that it was a relaxing social experience. Before and after the films were shown, people got a chance to talk with their neighbors or meet up with friends. A less social, but still incredibly popular, activity was listening to the radio. Nearly every home in America, even the least wealthy ones, had a radio in the 1930s.

Radio listeners during the Great Depression most frequently tuned in for music and news. Because television was not yet available, they also got to enjoy sitcoms, dramas, mysteries, detective shows, and other episodic programs similar to those later seen on TV. In fact, a number of popular radio shows, such as comedian Jack Benny's sitcom, became popular television programs in the 1950s. One of the most popular radio programs of the decade was the Amos 'n' Andy show, a nightly comedy about a big-city cab driver named Amos and his friend Andy, who regularly found themselves in humorous situations. More than 40 million people, roughly one-third of all Americans, listened to the show each night in 1931.

One thing that movies and radio had in common was that they cost money. People had to buy a ticket to see a movie or buy their own household radio. In an era in which money was scarce, many people tried to combine money-making

A Game of Chance in the Great Depression

One of the many games that people played in the 1930s to help them forget their troubles was bingo, which is still widely played today. The game was first recorded in 1778 and went by the name lotto (because it is a game of chance similar to a lottery). Several other early name variations were: keno, tombola, beano, and housy-housy. The man responsible for popularizing the game during the Great Depression was a New York toy salesman named Edwin Lowe. He came across the game, called beano, at a 1929 carnival. He reportedly played the game with some friends, and one of them spontaneously cried out "bingo!" when she won.

Bingo became popular during the Great Depression. All across America, people would play the game for fun.

Lowe realized that this was a catchy name, so he began printing sets of randomized cards and selling them to various organizations under the name "bingo." Lowe originally believed that bingo could be a new and effective way to earn money for churches or charities, but its nature as a gambling game made it widely popular. It was an immediate success in the United States. Not only was it a fun, exciting way to pass the time, it was also possible to easily win money. Lowe's company also went on to manufacture Yahtzee, another popular American game.

with their leisure activities. Gambling, including games such as blackjack and other casino-type games were extremely popular, for example. People also liked to bet on the outcomes of pinball games, as pinball machines were first

Jack Benny was one of America's most prominent comedians during the Depression. His radio shows provided millions of people a brief escape from the terrible conditions of the decade.

introduced in the United States in the early 1930s.

Another way that people tried to both have fun and strike it rich at the same time was by participating in dance marathons. As their name implies, these were public competitions in which numerous couples began dancing at a given signal. The object was to see which couple could continue dancing the longest without falling asleep or collapsing onto the dance floor. Eventually, dancers would drop out from sheer exhaustion, until, after days, only one couple was left. Some of these marathons could last for more than two or three days straight. Prizes at the larger dance contests ran from several hundred up to several thousand dollars. These rewards were huge during the Great Depression and would allow marathon dancers to feed their families or pay their rent.

The less glamorous aspects of dance marathons were that the participants risked their health and even their lives. With no sleep and without regular meals for days on end, many became sick, and it is reported that some people even died. As a result, by the late 1930s, most states had outlawed these contests. These fanatical public spectacles were a symptom of the hard times of the Depression, when many people were willing to do almost anything to temporarily forget their troubles—especially if it could make them some extra money.

Chapter Six

HARD LIVES MADE EVEN HARDER

Nearly every American alive in the 1930s suffered as a result of the Great Depression. Its economic destruction affected everyone, from the richest of society to the poorest and everyone in between. Much of the focus of the Depression, however, is on men who lost their jobs. This is because, in the early 20th century, men made up an overwhelming majority of the workforce. Women were almost always homemakers, meaning they typically stayed at home and supported their husband and children. American society in the 1930s believed that this was the natural order of things: Men worked, while women took care of them. For this reason, women were often regarded as less important than men.

The same was true of a wide variety of minority groups. Blacks, Native Americans, European immigrants, migrant workers, and other groups of people struggled against widespread prejudice and discrimination. Even before the Depression hit, these groups, as well as white women, had difficulty getting ahead in life. White men were unquestionably the dominant class, and they wanted to stay that way. When the financial ruin of the Depression hit, these groups were affected just as severely as white men.

President Roosevelt and his New Deal tried to institute programs and initiatives that would aid these underprivileged groups. Though there was some social progress towards equality—the most famous instance being Frances Perkins, the first female cabinet member in U.S. history—many of these plans failed to make much of an impact. With the weight of the Great Depression bearing down on every American, the dominant class was generally able to maintain its major share of power.

High-Powered Women

Despite the significant obstacles, some members of these minority groups were able to make some measurable gains during the 1930s. In the case of American women, these gains were often ceremonial or formal appointments by the president to various governmental posts. Generally, these positions were high in rank and highly visible. In addition to Frances Perkins, the first female U.S. cabinet member, they included Ruth Bryan Owen, the first female ambassador; Marion Glass Banister, the first female assistant treasurer of the United States; and Florence Allen, the first woman to preside as chief judge of a federal circuit court of appeals. Women were also in charge of some of the New Deal programs. Hallie Flanagan directed the Federal Theatre Project, for instance, and Mary McLeod Bethune held a high position in the National Youth Administration. Bethune was also the first black American to serve in such a high position in a federal government agency.

The most visible woman in the government during the Depression era was the First Lady of the United States, Eleanor Roosevelt. As one historian explained, Eleanor did a great deal to advance the status of American women:

> *[Her] commitment to women's full … participation in American politics and business was intense, and she worked with women's groups around the nation to build their political base … In her first year as First Lady, [she] worked hard to keep women involved in establishing and evaluating the New Deal … [She] assembled a list of women qualified for executive level appointments, urged the Roosevelt administration to hire them, and, when their suggestions did not get a fair hearing, did not hesitate to take their ideas [directly] to FDR.*[66]

Frances Perkins was one of the most powerful women in the United States during the Depression. She accomplished a great deal for both women and minority groups.

Outside of these high positions, however, the progress for women in America was not as advanced. In fact, the vast majority of American women made only small gains against widespread prejudices during the 1930s. This was partly because of longstanding social traditions that viewed men as the main breadwinners and heads of households. One component of this prejudice was the gender-typing of jobs. Gender-typing is when certain jobs are perceived as "masculine," such as manufacturing, and some as "feminine," such as clerical work. During the Great Depression, American manufacturing industries sustained major damage, and that put men out of work. However, because women worked in other industries, commonly as receptionists or secretaries, their jobs were more stable. Between 1930 and 1940, in fact, the total employment of women actually increased. For this reason, some people thought that working women were taking jobs away from men, and thereby hurting both their families and the country.

This sexist attitude explains why a 1936 Gallup poll indicated that 82 percent of Americans believed employers should discriminate against married women. Another survey, conducted in 1939, "showed that 84 percent of insurance companies, 65 percent of banks, and 63 percent of [public utility companies] had restrictions on married women working."[67] Some men were particularly hostile toward female employment. "Simply fire the women, who shouldn't be working anyway, and hire the men," journalist Norman Cousins wrote. "Presto! No unemployment. No relief rolls. No Depression."[68]

Trouble Gaining Traction

The reality was not always so simple a matter as women filling jobs that men used to do. Women almost exclusively did work that men did not traditionally do. This was also work that many men would have refused to do, even if they had to remain out of a job and stand in breadlines instead. One-fifth of all female workers during the Depression era were maids or other domestic servants, for example. In the 1930s, live-in maids made the low wage of $8 a week in New York City, which was the highest paying area in the country for domestic workers. Elsewhere, the weekly salary would have been even less.

Furthermore, the few women who were employed to do jobs that men were willing to take made considerably less money for the same kind and quality of work. The average annual pay of an employed woman in the 1930s was $525, compared with $1,027 for a man. Even many of FDR's New Deal programs, including those headed by women, discriminated against women by failing to grant them pay equal to that of men. While wage-earning codes set by the NRA did help women workers by guaranteeing them a minimum wage, the minimum wage was not equal across the sexes. The minimum for men was much higher than the minimum for women.

In the early 1900s, women were largely domestic servants, similar to this maid. Though some unemployed men were angry that women had jobs, they were not willing to do the same work.

Even though women's employment increased during the Depression, working women were still the minority. Many stayed home to cook, clean, raise children, work in fields, and do the best they could to make ends meet in the cruel economy. Though these women had done nothing to threaten the male job market, they were nonetheless victimized by deeply ingrained gender biases. The Social Security Act initially treated women unfairly, for example. When it was first enacted, the program helped only the wage earners themselves, who were almost always the men. If a male worker died, his stay-at-home wife could not collect any of his benefits and found herself shut out of the system. Even when the government amended the law in 1939, unemployed widows were only permitted to collect a certain percentage of their deceased husbands' benefits.

Whether they worked or not, American women in the 1930s were still widely considered second-class citizens. They

Women struggled just as much as men during the Depression. Some women had to take care of their children by themselves, as their husbands either died or deserted them.

An Educator and Administrator

One of the leading black American figures of the 1920s and 1930s was Mary McLeod Bethune. She was born in South Carolina in 1875 to two former slaves who had been freed at the close of the Civil War. A brilliant and hard-working student, she attended Scotia Seminary, a college in North Carolina. She soon earned a reputation as a high quality educator. In 1904, Bethune established a school in Daytona Beach, Florida, which eventually became Bethune-Cookman College. She served as president of the college from 1923 to 1942 and later from 1946 to 1947. Partly because of her friendship with First Lady Eleanor Roosevelt, FDR placed Bethune in charge of the division of Negro affairs in a New Deal program, the National Youth Administration (NYA). This made Bethune the first black American to hold a head position in a government agency. In 1935, she founded the National Council of Negro Women, an organization dedicated to the advancement of black women in America. Bethune died in 1955. She is remembered today not only for her achievements as an educator, but also because she broke down racial and gender barriers in the federal government.

undoubtedly benefited to some degree from the New Deal, but in general, their lives were only improved minimally. Issues of gender equality took a place of lesser importance in the face of economic catastrophe. One historical scholar described this trend:

> *In the face of a collective mood that [encouraged] women's domestic ties and [discouraged] working women, the feminist ideals that had grown during earlier periods lost momentum. Already waning during the 1920s, feminist sentiments [weakened] further during the Great Depression due to pressing economic concerns. Groups that had supported women's rights ... remained in the political background during the 1930s.*[69]

A Powerful Prejudice

One of the other most prominent minorities to suffer from general prejudice during the Great Depression was the black population—both men and women—in the United States. America was not even 100 years removed from the Civil War, which abolished slavery, and old discriminatory practices were still in place, especially in the South. African

Americans were almost always considered inferior to whites.

At the height of the Depression, when jobs were few and far between, many racist whites resented seeing blacks get any kind of work. These whites believed that they should have the first pick of all jobs. Similarly to women, before the onset of the Depression, black citizens frequently did jobs that many white men would not take or did not want. Some of these undesirable positions were domestic servant, elevator operator, garbage collector, waiter, street cleaner, and train porter. When the economy collapsed, more whites were willing to take these jobs, if they were even available, and demanded that blacks quit or be fired to make way for them. Some white people in Atlanta, Georgia began using the racially discriminatory slogan: "No jobs for [blacks] until every white man has a job."[70] Prejudice such as this was widespread and only made worse by the Depression.

One result of such blatant racism was that Depression-era blacks were, more often than not, the last to get hired and the first to get fired. Their employment opportunities were virtually nonexistent,

A large proportion of black Americans worked as sharecroppers during the Great Depression.

Unfounded Fears

One white man who lived through the Depression was shocked by the open racism of his fellow Americans when he traveled to the South to help the government build a camp for poor black people. He remembered some of the prejudicial remarks he overheard before the camp was constructed:

> *When the government came in and started to build a model camp for Negroes, with screened shelters and shower baths and flush toilets, and an infirmary, a community center, a school and playgrounds … [local whites] raised hell. What was the government's idea anyway, ruining the rental value of they [homes]? … the Negroes wouldn't use the camp, [the whites argued]. They liked to be dirty; they liked to be diseased; they liked to be vicious.*
>
> *When the [whites] saw that the government was going ahead anyway, they said: You'll have to hire a bunch of camp guards, white guards, and have them control the camp with clubs and pistols or the Negroes won't pay the rent. Or they'll stop working entirely and they'll take the camp to pieces.*[1]

The racially motivated fears of these white protestors were unfounded. When the government did open the camp for homeless black Americans, its new, all-black governing council ran it efficiently and well.

1. Quoted in Studs Terkel, *Hard Times: An Oral History of the Great Depression*. New York, NY: Random House, 2000, p. 280.

and any job they managed to land was highly unstable. In 1932, with the country's overall unemployment figure nearing 25 percent, the unemployment rate for blacks was already 50 percent. At the start of the 1930s, a large portion of America's 12 million black citizens lived in rural areas, and millions worked in agricultural jobs. Less than 15 percent of black farmers then owned the land they worked on. The vast majority were sharecroppers, meaning they worked on someone else's land in exchange for a portion of the profits.

As in most American industries in the Depression, agricultural production fell on hard times, and many landowners evicted their tenants. Because such a large portion of the black population worked as sharecroppers, their sudden job loss was a huge blow to national unemployment averages. Moreover, even the African Americans who kept their agricultural jobs were paid less money than whites in similar jobs. In 1934, black farmers had an average income of $200 or less per year; this was not nearly enough to live a good life and far less money than white farmers earned.

Roosevelt's secretary of the interior, Harold Ickes, was a prominent advocate for more racial equality in the United States. He wrote, "The Negro [black man] has met with many abuses and obstacles ... For generations, he has been exploited by corrupt politicians, who have bought his vote or have made him promises which were never expected to be kept."[71] Nate Shaw, a black Alabama cotton farmer, was more blunt: "[The] colored man [has] just been a dog for this country for years and years,"[72] he said.

A New Deal for African Americans?

Though racism, prejudice, and discrimination against African Americans were still strong during the Depression, there was some major progress toward racial equality during the 1930s. Under some of FDR's New Deal programs in the middle of the decade, blacks made more economic and social gains than they had in the entire six decades following the Civil War. These gains were still not enough to eliminate prejudice by any means; when the Depression ended in the early 1940s, blacks were still second-class citizens suffering under an enormous load of racial discrimination. However, it was because of Roosevelt's administration and the New Deal that the idea of black equality stepped onto a major national stage in America. Some historians trace the beginnings of the Civil Rights movement, which blossomed in the 1950s and 1960s, back to the mid-1930s.

Though many of FDR's top advisers supported more equal rights for blacks, it is still unclear what FDR personally thought about blacks. In his public speeches and policies, he at least attempted to treat black Americans more fairly, more equally, and with more dignity than they had been accorded in the past. Roosevelt abolished segregation in federal offices in Washington, D.C., and began to racially integrate the armed forces. He also appointed black men and women as advisers on race relations in the main offices of several New Deal programs.

The president made these moves, which were revolutionary during the 1930s, partly because he had surrounded himself with progressive, fair-minded individuals, such as Ickes. They advised him politically, but Roosevelt's attitudes about race relations and equality were influenced even more by his wife. Eleanor Roosevelt became a staunch advocate for the rights of American minorities, including blacks. Many of her tolerant attitudes and her knowledge about black problems came from her close friendship with Mary McLeod Bethune, who long served as one of FDR's chief advisers on minority issues. The first lady also learned a great deal about the struggles of black Americans from another black friend, Walter White. He was a leader of the National Association for the Advancement of Colored People (NAACP), which had been established in 1909. Some historical reports indicate that Eleanor was responsible for bringing the need for equality to FDR's attention. She is also credited with convincing Roosevelt to make his New Deal programs more inclusive of minority groups.

As a result, many of FDR's job programs, such as the PWA and CCC, became small, but still important, instruments of equality. These agencies mandated equal pay for equal work, even across racial boundaries. Many whites complained about this equal treatment, and argued that their labor was worth more than the labor of black men. Advocates for equality responded by pointing out that black workers had to support their families just as white

Eleanor Roosevelt, shown here meeting with officials from the NAACP, was one of the most outspoken advocates for more equal rights for African Americans during this era.

workers did, and how could blacks be expected to have a decent life if they made far less money than whites? Roosevelt responded to racist remarks and demands by employing hundreds of thousands of black men through the CCC and appointing a number of other minorities to high-ranking positions throughout his New Deal initiatives.

African Americans also benefited from loans obtained from the Farm Security Administration (FSA), a New Deal agency that lent money to needy farmers. Nearly a quarter of the FSA's loans went to blacks. "One could argue," historian Raymond Wolters wrote, "that even this share was inadequate because the Negro's needs were so much greater" than those of whites. "It is nevertheless a tribute to the fair-mindedness of the FSA's administrators that Negroes received as large a share … as they did."[73]

Though some of these changes were undoubtedly positive, they were still relatively small victories for black Americans. Racism was still alive and well in the United States, no matter how much Roosevelt and his chief administrators tried to avoid it. Blacks were abused in hiring, firing, wages, housing, and other areas. New Deal administrators typically responded to criticisms of these abuses by saying that the fault lay with the old prejudices of individuals, not with Roosevelt's government. Even the most progressive minds in the federal government realized that centuries of prejudice could not be dismantled overnight. They did everything possible, however, to diminish racial discrimination where they could.

Overlooked Native Americans

Longstanding prejudices against Native Americans, commonly called American Indians in the 1930s, were also impossible to erase quickly. Government officials did, however, make attempts to better integrate Native Americans into mainstream society. When the Depression hit, many of them had already been confined to reservations for several decades. During those years, the federal government had been pursuing a policy of assimilation: slowly trying to absorb Native Americans into white society and thereby eradicate traditional Native American culture. The policy was poorly applied, was not very successful, and actually intensified prejudice against Native Americans. The government commissioned reports on Native American affairs and was aware that neither Native Americans nor white Americans were learning to get along. Native Americans were just as devastated as everyone else when the Great Depression hit.

This situation fortunately began to improve in 1933, when the Roosevelt administration launched the New Deal. John Collier, an open-minded and progressive social worker, became the U.S. Commissioner of Indian Affairs. Collier recognized that the assimilation policy was racist and destructive, and launched a new policy that aimed to preserve traditional Native

American cultures. This goal was the central feature of the 1934 Indian Reorganization Act (IRA). It strengthened tribal governments, encouraged the expansion of Native American commercial endeavors to create self-reliance, and helped secure education loans for potential scholars.

Despite its positive goals, the IRA was aimed mostly at the long term; in the middle of the Depression, many Native Americans simply needed jobs. With this in mind, Collier organized the Indian Emergency Conservation Work (IECW) program, funded as a branch of the CCC. Thousands of Native Americans were employed on or near reservations to plant forests, combat soil erosion, and build roads and fire lookout stations. Though it was enacted at a much smaller scale than the general CCC, the IECW was highly successful among unemployed and impoverished Native Americans in the 1930s.

Other Minority Groups

While Native Americans struggled to support their families and preserve their culture from mainstream America, immigrant minorities were also experiencing prejudice. In the three decades before the onset of the Depression, millions of immigrants had come to the United States from Italy, Greece, Poland, Hungary, Germany, Russia, and many other countries. They received a mixed reception from the American populace. Some people welcomed them, helping them assimilate and respecting their various international cultures. Others, however, saw them as intruders who were trying to steal jobs from "real Americans." This attitude intensified during the Depression, when jobs were extremely difficult to find for members of any ethnicity. A number of immigrants—and even their American-born children—were the targets of fierce racial discrimination all across the United States. This could range from children calling each other racially offensive names to murder.

Even some whites who were not immigrants were discriminated against during the Depression, based partially on the fear that they were trying to take other people's jobs. The so-called Oakies were the most famous example. They were the principal victims of the Dust Bowl, a series of disastrous dust storms in the 1930s that ravaged the Great Plains of America. More than 500,000 citizens of the region fled to other states. An estimated 15 percent of Oklahomans, along with people from other states affected by the Dust Bowl, moved to California. Although not all the migrants were from Oklahoma, they all collectively became known as Oakies, which soon became a derogatory term. "They were promptly stereotyped, exactly like a racial minority," editor and writer Carey McWilliams, himself the child of migrant workers in the 1930s, later remembered. "They were [supposedly] shiftless and lazy and irresponsible and had too many children … Once I went into the foyer of this third-rate [movie theater] in

Oakies in Art

John Steinbeck is one of America's most famous novelists. He is known for writing extensively on the lives of migrant workers, such as he did in *The Grapes of Wrath*. This excerpt outlines some of the struggles faced by the Americans who were called Oakies in the 1930s:

> *And then the dispossessed were drawn west—from Kansas, Oklahoma, Texas, New Mexico; from Nevada and Arkansas families, tribes, dusted out, tractored out. Carloads, caravans, homeless and hungry; twenty thousand and fifty thousand and a hundred thousand and two hundred thousand. They streamed over the mountains, hungry and restless … The kids are hungry. We got no place to live. Like ants scurrying for work, for food, and most of all for land … the migrants, flowed into California, two hundred and fifty thousand, and three hundred thousand. Behind them … [other] tenants were being forced off [their land]. And new waves were on the way, new waves of the dispossessed and the homeless, hardened, intent, and dangerous.*[1]

1. John Steinbeck, *The Grapes of Wrath*. New York, NY: Viking Press, 1939, pp. 317–318.

[California] and I saw a sign: Negroes and Oakies upstairs."[74]

The plight of migrant workers was etched into America's cultural consciousness by John Steinbeck's 1939 novel *The Grapes of Wrath* and by the movie version made shortly afterward. Both showed how poor migrant workers experienced intense poverty and prejudice during the Depression years. To their surprise and sadness, they found themselves among the minority groups that frequently suffered more than the rest of the country during the worst economic disaster in history.

Epilogue

FORWARD FROM THE DEPRESSION

As President Franklin Roosevelt's first term was coming to a close in 1936, he was the undisputed favorite to win that year's election. Though unemployment was still high, poverty was widespread, and there was no clear-cut conclusion in sight for the Great Depression, Americans had a general sense that his New Deal was the best option moving forward. His critics argued that the government was growing inappropriately large, and his programs were only partially successful. His supporters responded that unemployment had decreased by almost 10 percent since he took office, and the government needed to get involved to save the economy and get it back on the right track.

As a result, FDR won his second term almost unopposed, and his victory remains one of the largest margins of victory in U.S. history. During his next four years, his administration worked to refine and broaden existing New Deal programs, while introducing new and diverse initiatives. Though he did not single-handedly end the Great Depression, the path to recovery looked clearer every day. He won an unprecedented third consecutive presidential election in 1940—the only person to have ever done so. Entering this third term, FDR and his advisers were looking for a new way to end the economic crisis. Though the New Deal's programs had been functioning as promised for six years, unemployment was still high (though still decreasing), and the economy was still recuperating. A new world war would change that.

A Bloody Stimulus

One of the reasons for the steadily declining unemployment rate was an increase in manufacturing production. Beginning around 1939, most of Europe had been plunged into World War II. Though the United States was not yet directly involved, it began supplying Britain and its other allies with large amounts of industrial and military equipment. As the war went on, production requirements increased. This created many new jobs for Americans in the process. By 1941, the level of industrial production in the United States was even higher than it had been early in 1929, before the stock market crashed and set off the Great Depression. American industrial output continued to grow exponentially higher after the Japanese attack on Pearl Harbor in December 1941, which pulled the United States fully into the ongoing world war. Building up the nation's armed forces was an extremely powerful catalyst for economic recovery.

Under these circumstances, the question for economists and historians became: How much did the New Deal itself contribute to the national return to prosperity? Some experts have concluded that Roosevelt's policies and programs to fight the Depression were failures. They argue that he conducted a large, expensive, and ultimately ineffective experiment. In their view, he and his New Dealers continually failed to balance the federal budget, greatly increased the national debt, and expanded the federal

After the United States was pulled into World War II, producing military goods became a top priority. The armed forces rushed to prepare for a long conflict.

This poster, which encouraged all Americans, especially women, to contribute to the country's war effort, is one of the lasting symbols of the early 1940s.

government into an inappropriately huge bureaucracy. Other historians have been more positive in their analysis of the New Deal. They have argued that its various programs helped increase the national average income and employed millions of jobless, desperate people. Most importantly, Roosevelt and the New Deal restored the country's morale, which had reached an all-time low during the Depression's early years.

Moreover, Roosevelt's defenders have pointed out that there is no way to tell what the New Deal might have accomplished if the war had not erupted. Joe Marcus, a prominent economist in the 1930s, said, "The war did end the Depression. That doesn't mean that something else might not have ended it."[75] In fact, Marcus and other experts have argued that it is possible a few more years of vigorous, costly New Deal programs might have brought the economy back on track. It is true that the government borrowed a lot of the money to fund its New Deal projects, which created an enormous budget deficit. Similarly, however, the government borrowed a great deal of money to fund its costly war effort, which also created a deficit. The difference, as McElvaine pointed out, was in the scale of the borrowing and spending:

> *The military buildup of 1940–41 did more to revive American industry and reduce unemployment than had any New Deal program. This is not, though, the criticism of Roosevelt's policies that it might seem. It simply means that the deficit-spending … approach that the New Deal had used timidly worked when employed boldly. Rather than representing a reversal of the New Deal prescription, the military spending of 1940 and subsequent years represented a much larger dose of the same medicine.*[76]

Providing for the Public

Regardless of the immediate results of the New Deal, there is no doubt that the Depression and FDR's programs have impacted the United States in significant and enduring ways. His reforms were revolutionary at the time, his programs were bold, and his strategies were unique. He served as president for more years than anyone else, and the public perception of his New Deal initiatives was a major factor in his three reelections.

In the long run, various large-scale social programs, including Social Security, remained in place, and they have become accepted fixtures of American life. Not long after America escaped from the Great Depression, politicians from both major parties, Democrats and Republicans, accepted many of the bold and formerly controversial components of the New Deal, including laws for minimum wages, weekly work hours, and the insurance of bank deposits. In the 21st century, some of these topics have come up for debate among politicians again; however, many programs are still widely supported by the American public.

Before the beginning of the Depression and the creation of the New Deal to fight it, the United States had no national old-age pension plan, no aid to dependent children, no federal housing, no federal compensation for the unemployed, no federal school lunch program for children from low-income families, no minimum wage requirements, and no government welfare system. Today, even the most conservative political figures believe that at least a minimum level of government aid is required to help those citizens who are in major and immediate need. The New Deal laid the groundwork and provided the basic ideals and structure for that aid. As historian Anthony Badger described,

> *New Deal welfare programs gave the unemployed money and jobs. The lasting loyalty of low-income voters to Roosevelt expressed their appreciation of the very real and essential benefits they received ... The New Deal welfare programs provided direct assistance to perhaps as many as 35 percent of the population. It bequeathed [passed on] a commitment to a minimum level of social welfare from which successive governments have never been entirely able to escape.*[77]

One of the major changes in the New Deal was the elimination of child labor. It also prohibited sweatshops that exploited men, women, and children by grossly underpaying them and forcing them to work in substandard conditions. These new laws were beneficial to low-income Americans, both immediately and in the long term.

Most of the New Deal programs that still exist in some form as of 2017 are part of the national economy. The 1933 Securities Act, for example, made company heads criminally liable for misinformation in their financial statements. The 1934 Securities and Exchange Act established a federal commission to oversee the stock market; this helps prevent another massive stock market crash such as the one in 1929. Also created in 1934, the Federal Housing Administration (FHA) made one aspect of the American dream more accessible: owning a home. The FHA is a government organization that helps potential homeowners get access to mortgages or other loans that are more affordable than what banks offer. Because widespread home ownership is an important component of a thriving national economy, the FHA has been successful for more than 80 years.

America Restored

The most obvious effects of the Great Depression were visible and material. People lost their jobs, they went hungry, and they were forced to live on the streets. The millions of people who lived below the poverty line can be expressed with numbers. These statistics, however, cannot tell the entire story of the difficult 1930s in America. Alongside the national economic Depression rose a sort of national psychological depression: People lost hope in themselves, their leaders, and their country. For years, especially from 1929 to 1932, it seemed like there was no end in sight for millions of struggling Americans. When President Franklin D. Roosevelt took office, things began to change.

The historical significance of the New Deal is impossible to ignore. Regardless of whether or not the programs worked to stimulate the economy, FDR's administration introduced hope back into the general American populace. Millions of people were put back to work, and they could suddenly provide for their families again. He bolstered the country's belief in itself, which had been a core component of the national spirit dating all the way back to the American Revolution. Roosevelt's administration reminded the nation that Americans could rise to any challenge—and overcome it—just as their forefathers did. One historian wrote, "The New Deal had taken up a people brought to the brink of despair by poverty and failure and had restored their morale … [it restored] belief that a democratic people could cope with its own problems in a democratic way."[78]

Though the 1930s are remembered most as a time of great adversity, it is equally important to recognize the strength of the American spirit. The stock market crash of 1929 instigated what may go down as the worst economic crisis in national history, millions of people went hungry and homeless, and it took a world war to get the United States back on track financially. Once it began to recover in 1939, however, America never stopped. It rose from the depths of economic ruin to become one of the most powerful countries in the world—a position it has held ever since. President Roosevelt played a major part in this revitalization. As historian Arthur M. Schlesinger wrote,

> *Roosevelt [equipped] the [Democratic] party with a philosophy of government intervention—a belief, as he put it, that "the government has the definite duty to use all its power and resources to meet the new social problems with new social controls." Much of the New Deal was imperfect … But the shortcomings of the New Deal vanish in the general perspective of its supreme success: that is, in the restoration of America as a fighting faith, and in the restoration of democracy as a workable way of life … The New Deal took a broken and despairing land and gave it new confidence in itself.*[79]

Notes

Introduction: A Disaster

1. John C. Chalberg, "Introduction," in William Dudley, ed., *The Great Depression: Opposing Viewpoints*. San Diego, CA: Greenhaven Press, 1994, p. 14.
2. Katharine D. Lumpkin and Dorothy W. Douglas, *Child Workers in America*. New York, NY: Robert M. McBride, 1937, p. 4.
3. Quoted in Studs Terkel, *Hard Times: An Oral History of the Great Depression*. New York, NY: Random House, 2000, p. 45.
4. Quoted in Robert McElvaine, *The Great Depression: America 1929–1941*. New York, NY: Random House, 1993, p. 174.
5. Quoted in Terkel, *Hard Times*, p. 46.
6. Quoted in Dudley, *The Great Depression*, p. 36.
7. Quoted in Howard Zinn, *A People's History of the United States*. New York, NY: HarperCollins, 2005, p. 379.
8. Quoted in McElvaine, *The Great Depression*, p. 175.
9. Quoted in McElvaine, *The Great Depression*, p. 174.
10. McElvaine, *The Great Depression*, p. xiii.

Chapter One: The Great Depression Begins

11. Zinn, *A People's History of the United States*, p. 373.
12. McElvaine, *The Great Depression*, p. 38.
13. Samuel E. Morison, *The Oxford History of the American People*. New York, NY: Oxford University Press, 1965, p. 937.
14. Edward R. Ellis, *A Nation in Torment: The Great Depression, 1929–1939*. New York, NY: Capricorn, 1970, p. 103.
15. Quoted in Terkel, *Hard Times*, p. 424.
16. Quoted in Terkel, *Hard Times*, p. 66.
17. Quoted in Terkel, *Hard Times*, p. 73.
18. Gerald W. Johnson, *Franklin D. Roosevelt: Portrait of a Great Man*. New York, NY: William Morrow, 1967, pp. 119–120.
19. Quoted in Terkel, *Hard Times*, p. 424.
20. Quoted in Terkel, *Hard Times*, p. 425.
21. Quoted in Terkel, *Hard Times*, p. 20.
22. Quoted in Morison, *The Oxford History of the American People*, p. 945.

Chapter Two: A Powerless President

23. Quoted in Morison, *The Oxford History of the American People*, p. 945.
24. T.H. Watkins, *The Great Depression:*

America in the 1930s. Boston, MA: Little, Brown and Company, 1993 p. 61.
25. Quoted in "Herbert Hoover," WhiteHouse.gov, Accessed January 28, 2017. www.whitehouse.gov/1600/presidents/herberthoover.
26. Quoted in "Herbert Hoover," WhiteHouse.gov.
27. Herbert Hoover, "Rugged Individualism Speech of October 22, 1928," in Richard Hofstadter, ed., *Great Issues in American History: A Documentary Record, Volume II, 1864–1957*. New York, NY: Vintage, 1960, pp. 338–339.
28. Herbert Hoover, "Rugged Individualism Speech of October 22, 1928."
29. Herbert Hoover, "Public vs. Private Financing of Relief Efforts," The American Presidency Project. www.presidency.ucsb.edu/ws/?pid=22932.
30. Quoted in Morison, *The Oxford History of the American People*, p. 946.
31. Quoted in Anthony J. Badger, *The New Deal: The Depression Years, 1933–1940*. New York, NY: Farrar, Straus and Giroux, 1989, p. 48.
32. Quoted in William E. Leuchtenburg, ed., *The New Deal: A Documentary History*. New York, NY: Harper and Row, 1968, p. 11.
33. Quoted in McElvaine, *The Great Depression*, p. 52.

Chapter Three: A New Leader

34. Franklin D. Roosevelt, "Address Accepting the Presidential Nomination at the Democratic National Convention in Chicago," The American Presidency Project. www.presidency.ucsb.edu/ws/?pid=75174.
35. Miller Center of Public Affairs, "Franklin D. Roosevelt: Impact and Legacy," University of Virginia, Accessed January 30, 2017. millercenter.org/president/biography/fdroosevelt-impact-and-legacy.
36. Franklin D. Roosevelt, "First Inaugural Address," in Halford Ross Ryan, ed., *The Inaugural Addresses of Twentieth-century American Presidents*. Westport, CT: Praeger Publishers, 1993, p. 97.
37. Quoted in Robert Lynn Fuller, *"Phantom of Fear": The Banking Panic of 1933*. Jefferson, NC: McFarland, 2012, p. 186.
38. Quoted in Franklin Delano Roosevelt, "First Fireside Chat: Delivered 12 March 1933, Washington D.C.," American Rhetoric. www.americanrhetoric.com/speeches/fdrfirstfiresidechat.html.
39. Franklin D. Roosevelt, "Letter of March 13, 1933 to John S. Lawrence," in Elliot Roosevelt, ed., *FDR: His Personal Letters, 1928–1945, Volume One*. New York, NY: Duell, Sloan and Pearce, 1950, pp. 338–339.
40. McElvaine, *The Great Depression*, p. 149.
41. Quoted in Wolfgang Schivelbusch, *Three New Deals: Reflections on Roosevelt's America, Mussolini's*

Italy, and Hitler's Germany. New York, NY: Metropolitan Books, 2006, p. 159.

42. Quoted in Terkel, *Hard Times*, p. 250.
43. Quoted in James MacGregor Burns, *The Workshop of Democracy: The American Spirit, Vol. 2*, New York, NY: Open Road Media, 2012.

Chapter Four: Programs for Recovery

44. Quoted in Terkel, *Hard Times*, pp. 247–248.
45. Quoted in Terkel, *Hard Times*, p. 267.
46. Quoted in Terkel, *Hard Times*, pp. 274–275.
47. Franklin D. Roosevelt, "Presidential Statement Upon Signing the Social Security Act, August 14, 1935," in *The Public Papers and Addresses of Franklin D. Roosevelt, Volume Four*. New York, NY: Random House, 1938, p. 324.
48. Quoted in Dudley, *The Great Depression*, p. 171.
49. Quoted in Arthur M. Schlesinger Jr., *The Coming of the New Deal*. Boston, MA: Houghton Mifflin, 1959, p. 311.
50. Frances Perkins, "The Social Security Act," in Leutchenburg, *The New Deal*, pp. 85–86.
51. McElvaine, *The Great Depression*, pp. 158–159.
52. Quoted in Terkel, *Hard Times*, p. 249.
53. McElvaine, *The Great Depression*, p. 159.
54. Don Nardo, *Franklin D. Roosevelt: U.S. President*. New York, NY: Chelsea House, 1996, p. 74.
55. Franklin D. Roosevelt, "Fireside Chat 9: On 'Court-Packing' (March 9, 1937)," University of Virginia. millercenter.org/president/speeches/speech-3309.
56. Quoted in Leutchenburg, *The New Deal*, p. 214.

Chapter Five: Life in Uncertain Times

57. Lorena A. Hickok, *One Third of a Nation: Lorena Hickok Reports on the Great Depression*. Chicago, IL: University of Illinois Press, 1983, pp. 56–57.
58. Lorena A. Hickok, *One Third of a Nation*, p. 60.
59. McElvaine, *The Great Depression*, pp. 172–173.
60. Quoted in McElvaine, *The Great Depression*, p. 172.
61. Quoted in McElvaine, *The Great Depression*, p. 173.
62. Quoted in Dudley, *The Great Depression*, pp. 34–35.
63. Quoted in Badger, *The New Deal*, p. 11.
64. McElvaine, *The Great Depression*, pp. 340–341.
65. Quoted in McElvaine, *The Great Depression*, p. 173–174.

Chapter Six: Hard Lives Made Even Harder

66. The Eleanor Roosevelt Papers Project Editors, "Eleanor Roosevelt and the Women's Movement," The Eleanor Roosevelt Papers Project. www2.gwu.edu/~erpapers/teachinger/lesson-plans/notes-er-and-womens-movement.cfm.
67. Quoted in Mary Eleanor Triece, *On the Picket Line: Strategies of Working-Class Women during the Depression*. Chicago, IL: University of Illinois Press, 2007, p. 79.
68. Quoted in McElvaine, *The Great Depression*, p. 182.
69. Lisa Krissoff Boehm, "Women, Impact of the Great Depression on," *Encyclopedia of the Great Depression, vol. 2*, Robert S. McElvaine, ed. Macmillan Reference USA, 2004, pp. 1050–1055.
70. Quoted in McElvaine, *The Great Depression*, p. 187.
71. Harold L. Ickes, "The Negro as a Citizen," in Howard Zinn, ed., *New Deal Thought*. Indianapolis, IN: Bobbs Merrill, 1966, p. 341.
72. Quoted in Theodore Rosengarten, *All God's Dangers: The Life of Nate Shaw*. New York, NY: Knopf, 1974, p. 300.
73. Raymond Wolters, "The New Deal and the Negro," in John Braeman, Robert H. Bremner, and David Brody, ed., *The New Deal*. Columbus, OH: Ohio State University Press, 1975, p. 176.
74. Quoted in Terkel, *Hard Times*, p. 243.

Epilogue: Forward from the Depression

75. Quoted in Terkel, *Hard Times*, p. 269.
76. McElvaine, *The Great Depression*, p. 320.
77. Badger, *The New Deal*, p. 301.
78. Hofstadter, *The United States*, pp. 674–675.
79. Arthur M. Schlesinger Jr., "The Broad Accomplishments of the New Deal," in Edwin C. Rozwenc, ed., *The New Deal: Revolution or Evolution?*. Boston, MA: D.C. Heath, 1949, p. 101.

For More Information

Books

Crafts, N.R.F and Peter Fearon, eds. *The Great Depression of the 1930s: Lessons For Today*. Oxford, UK: Oxford University Press, 2013.
This informative book contains opinions and analysis by experts in economics, connecting the Great Depression to the 21st century.

Eichengreen, Barry J. *Hall of Mirrors: The Great Depression, the Great Recession, and the Uses—and Misuses—of History*. New York, NY: Oxford University Press, 2015.
This book draws parallels between the Great Depression of the 1930s and the so-called Great Recession, which occurred in 2008, outlining the similarities between each event.

Hanes, Sharon M., and Richard C. Hanes. *Great Depression and New Deal: Primary Sources*. Farmington Hills, MI: Gale, 2003.
This book is a useful collection of original sources relating to the Great Depression; it provides documentary accounts of the Depression era.

Levey, Richard H. *Dust Bowl!* New York, NY: Bearport, 2005.
The Dust Bowl occurred almost simultaneously with the Great Depression, and this book connects the two events.

Shlaes, Amity. *The Forgotten Man: A New History of the Great Depression*. New York, NY: HarperCollins, 2007.
This book, written from an economic point of view, gives some personal stories and details from the Great Depression.

Terkel, Studs. *Hard Times: An Oral History of the Great Depression*. New York, NY: Random House, 2000.
Studs Terkel is one of the most well-respected scholars and reporters of the Depression, and this book gives an in-depth look of the 1930s from a personal perspective.

Websites

Dear Mrs. Roosevelt (newdeal.feri.org/eleanor/)
This site links young researchers to letters sent to and from First Lady Eleanor Roosevelt, who played an important part during the Great Depression.

The Great Depression (www.history.com/topics/great-depression)
Maintained by the History Channel, this website gives an informative overview of the Depression and also has links to related videos and other pages.

"The Great Depression Was Ended by the End of World War II, Not the Start of It"
(www.forbes.com/sites/peterferrara/2013/11/30/the-great-depression-was-ended-by-the-end-of-world-war-ii-not-the-start-of-it/#77ceadc761cb)
This article outlines the controversial opinion that World War II did not immediately repair America's economy, and it gives sources to outline this argument.

A Photo Essay on the Great Depression
(www.english.illinois.edu/maps/depression/photoessay.htm)
This page is supported by the University of Illinois at Urbana-Champaign and contains numerous interesting and engaging photographs of the Great Depression, as well as descriptions of each picture.

Timeline of the Great Depression
(www.pbs.org/wgbh/american-experience/features/timeline/rails-timeline/)
This timeline is a detailed account of the important events of the decade of the Great Depression.

Index

Picture Credits

Cover, pp. 12, 23, 28, 30, 34, 35, 61, 72, 77 Bettmann/Contributor/Bettmann/Getty Images; pp. 4–5, 7 (top right), 7 (bottom), 10, 18, 24, 40, 43, 47, 60, 65, 88 Everett Historical/Shutterstock.com; p. 6 (bottom left) Underwood Archives/Contributor/Archive Photos/Getty Images; pp. 6 (bottom right), 11 FPG/Staff/Archive Photos/Getty Images; p. 7 (top left) National Archives/Handout/Hulton Archive/Getty Images; pp. 16, 76 PhotoQuest/Contributor/Archive Photos/Getty Images; p. 19 Bettmann/Contributor/Corbis Historical/Getty Images; p. 21 ullstein bild/Contributor/ullstein bild/Getty Images; p. 26 Spartan7W/Wikimedia Commons; p. 32 Courtesy of the Library of Congress; p. 38 Centpacrr/Wikimedia Commons; p. 45 Kamira/Shutterstock.com; p. 51 MPI/Stringer/Archive Photos/Getty Images; p. 54 neftali/Shutterstock.com; p. 55 ASSOCIATED PRESS/AP Photo; p. 68 H. Armstrong Roberts/Stringer/Retrofile/Getty Images; p. 69 Universal History Archive/Contributor/Universal Images Group/Getty Images; p. 71 Margaret Bourke-White/Contributor/The LIFE Picture Collection/Getty Images; p. 74 Keystone-France/Contributor/Gamma-Keystone/Getty Images; p. 79 Buyenlarge/Contributor/Archive Photos/Getty Images; p. 82 Library of Congress/Contributor/Corbis Historical/Getty Images; p. 87 Keystone/Staff/Hulton Archive/ Getty Images.

About the Author

After studying English literature in college, **Siyavush Saidian** became an editor and author of young adult nonfiction books in Buffalo, New York. He uses the wintry weather as an excuse to frequently stay inside and play video games with his fiancée, even in the summer. A self-professed nerd, he enjoys working with books from a wide range of topics.